ST
ED

150

YEARS OF POLICING IN MANCHESTER

150

150

2. Oldham Borough Police sports day at the turn of the century.

THE POLICE!

150 Years of Policing in the ManchesterArea

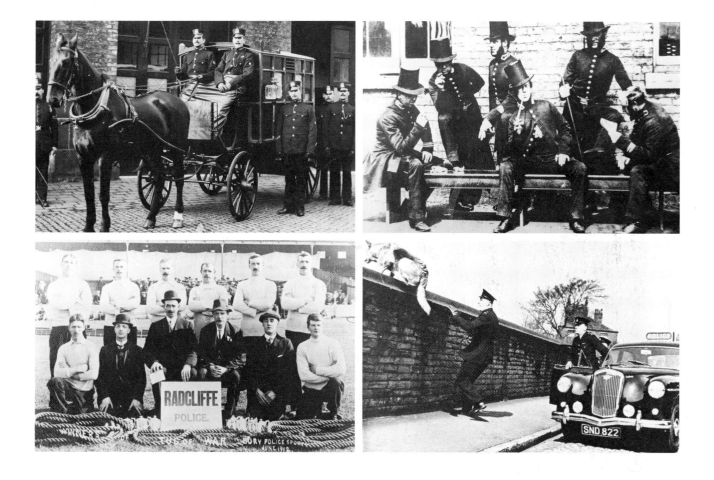

Archive Publications Ltd
By kind permission of the Chief Constable
Mr C JAMES ANDERTON, CBE, KStJ, QPM, DL, CBIM
Greater Manchester Police

PART PROCEEDS TO GMP COMMUNITY CHARITY ASSOCIATION

First published 1989 by
Archive Publications Ltd
10 Seymour Court
Manor Park
Runcorn
Cheshire WA7 1SY
in association with
Greater Manchester Police
Chester House
Boyer Street
Manchester M16 0RE

© 1989 Text Greater Manchester Police
© 1989 Photographs GMP and others as listed in acknowledgements
© 1989 Arrangement Archive Publications Ltd
Production by Richardson Press

ISBN: 0-948946-49-0

4. Escorting a Suffragettes' protest through Manchester.

CONTENTS

5. C James Anderton.

REFLECTIONS

FOREWORD FROM THE CHIEF CONSTABLE

"For preserving the peace by day and night and preventing robberies and other felonies and apprehending offenders against the peace..."

The principles on which the first police forces were founded in the last century still exist today and form the fundamental concept of policing by consent.

Although great changes have taken place in the last 150 years the police service of today, more than ever before, needs the public's full support and confidence in order to function properly.

This year commemorates a milestone in our history — 150 years of professional policing! A period which has seen massive changes in the social, environmental, cultural and technological framework of the country and nowhere more than in the Greater Manchester area. We have had to move with the times and rise to new challenges.

Communications have developed from the 'hue and cry', rattles and whistles to 99-channel hand-portable radios, cellular radio telephones and radar. Formal outfits of top-hat and tails have been replaced with today's functional uniforms of tunics, heavy-duty waterproof clothing — and even riot protection wear. Horses are no longer the main mode of police transport; instead we have modern traffic vehicles as well as the use of helicopters and light aircraft.

In 1839 Manchester followed the example of the Metropolitan Police and set about reorganising its police service to meet the needs of a rapidly-developing society. The inherent difficulties were fuelled by a bitter dispute over the legality of the City's Charter of Incorporation and until this crucial question was resolved the Government of the day decided to step in and appoint Sir Charles Shaw as Chief Commissioner of Manchester Police with full powers to organise, control and maintain the new force.

At that time Manchester Police numbered 357 officers and they covered an area which included Manchester, Ardwick, Bradford, Beswick, Cheetham, Chorlton-upon-Medlock, Harpurhey, Hulme and Newton. Together these townships had a population of some 187,000. By contrast, today's Greater Manchester Police force has an establishment of 6,943 covering a County population of around two and half million with the valued support of nearly 2,500 support staff and 500 Special Constables.

My own police career started in March 1953 as PC D52 in the Manchester Police stationed on the then 'D' Division covering the Hulme, Moss Side and South Manchester areas. I eventually left Manchester in 1967 as a chief inspector to take up a position as chief superintendent in the Cheshire Constabulary. After further service in Leicestershire and London I returned to Manchester in 1975 as Deputy Chief Constable.

I took over my present role as Chief Constable in July 1976 and can honestly say I have enjoyed my police career which now spans thirty-six years.

I feel deeply honoured to be the tenth Chief Constable of Manchester and to follow some great men whose efforts and foresight helped to make the force the magnificent organisation it is today. Officers such as Captain Edward Willis (1843-1857) Manchester's first locally-appointed Chief Constable who, despite early opposition, fought to obtain the acceptance and respect of the local populace for their first professional police force; Sir Robert Peacock (1898-1926) who introduced mounted police, educational classes for policemen and weekly rest days; Sir John Maxwell (1926-1942) who introduced policewomen into the force in 1940, and agreed the use of traffic lights, radio cars and motor patrols; and William James Richards (1966-1976) who introduced panda cars and personal radios.

Nor must we forget those of our Manchester police 'family' who went on to great things elsewhere; men such as Sir Robert Mark who served in Manchester between 1937 and 1956, rising to the rank of chief superintendent, and finally in 1972 became the Commissioner of the Metropolitan Police force in London.

I am proud and privileged to follow the great tradition and fine example of a tremendously professional body of men and women — police officers, Special Constabulary and civilian employees alike who work so hard in the service of the people of Greater Manchester. It is humbling and gratifying to know of the challenges which they face daily and overcome, often at great physical risk, and by which they earn the respect and gratitude, not just of myself and my senior officers, but of the community they serve. It is appropriate that I, on their behalf, should acknowledge the role of the Police Authority whose interest and support underpin GMP's success. They, like me, are in the fortunate position of being able to assist in the formulation of policies which will surely take this great force into the twenty-first century.

The future, then, still rests upon the principles of service to, and protection of, the public which form the force's motto.

C J Anderton, Esq, CBE, KSt J, QPM, DL, CBIM,
Chief Constable.

EARLY POLICING

Since the earliest times Britain has had a system of policing which, though primitive in its early stages, has developed into one of, if not the, finest police services in the world.

This development, however, did not happen overnight and numerous factors influenced its growth.

Various invaders from far-flung parts of the world introduced their own ideas of self-government but the same basic principles of keeping law and order and preserving the King or Queen's peace from the earliest times are still upheld today.

In this chapter a broad generalisation is given of the origins of policing in England, although it must be appreciated that local customs and practises may have varied in some of the areas now controlled by GMP.

The Emergence

One of the last invaders were the Anglo-Saxons who came to these shores in the middle of the sixth century. Bringing with them their own customs and laws, especially with regard to citizens and property, it was their belief that a crime was not only against the person but against the whole community and should be punished as such.

Men aged between twelve and sixty were collectively responsible for keeping the peace and they organised themselves into groups of ten families, each group called a 'tything' controlled by a 'tythingman', and each member ensured the good behaviour of his fellow men. If a crime was committed, it was the responsibility of the whole group to catch the offender and bring him to the court, or 'moot' as it was then known. Should they not catch him, the 'tything' itself had to be punished, usually by paying a fine.

When a crime was committed a witness would have to raise the alarm — then called hue and cry — to urge the

7. 'Hue and cry' in progress.

male villagers to join in the chase and bring him to justice.

As today, various courts existed which were used depending upon the seriousness of the offence. Minor offences would be dealt with by the local folk moot whilst the hundred court, under a hundredman or reeve, dealt with the more serious cases. The highest level of court for the whole area was the shire court headed by the shire reeve or sheriff.

6. At the centre of Anglo-Saxon justice was the folk moot presided over by the older men of the village.

2ND OCTOBER, 1612, TO 21ST OCTOBER, 1613.

	li	s	d
Itm̄ for makeinge of p̄cepts for hewe and Crye[1] after a yonge youthe[2] about 17 or 18 yeares of age for the takeinge of a darcke bay nagge out of the pasture of Robert Massye of Cowe lane in west-chester the 26th of Nouember 1612	o	o	8
Itm̄ for makeinge of p̄cepts for hewe and Crye the 12th daie of Aprill 1613 after such suspected psonns as had taken frome Richard Battid of Bameford iij peeces of Wollen Clothe forth of his Milne the 13th of Aprill 1613...	o	o	8
Itm̄ for makeinge of p̄ceptes for hewe and Cry the j th of Jannuarye 1612[-13] after Nicholas Harrisonne of Manchester blacke Smythe for suspiconne of Killinge Lawrance Massye of the same place ...	o	o	8
Itm̄ for makeinge of p̄cepts for hewe and Crye the xiiij th daye of August 1613 for one Robert Howorthe of Ratchdall Sheareman whoe wounded one Abrahame Butterworthe of Hundersfeild wythin the same Countye of Lanc̄ husbandmane	o	o	8
Itm̄ for makeinge of p̄cepts for hue and Crye the 23 of June 1613 after John Trauis Showmaker whoe had wounded one John Rothwell of Boulton and was ffledd	o	o	8
Itm̄ fo[r] makeinge of p̄cepts for hewe and Crye the xxviij th of June 1613 for the app̄hendinge of James Beeseleye and soe to bring him to the gayole at Lanc[aster] for his Misdemeano͛ ...	o	o	8

8. From the hue and cry to cords for tying up the prisoners ... all expenditure was recorded in the constable's accounts.

The Norman invasion, beginning with the Battle of Hastings in 1066, led to an alien and often harsh life-style suffered by the beleaguered Saxons, although the severity diminished in time. The accepted law-making and court systems were retained because the Normans recognised their efficiency, and it was the duty of the Norman sheriffs to ensure membership of the tythings was maintained to monitor good behaviour and uphold the court system.

Eventually local lords of the manor took over from the

9. Unlike courts of today the manor court often resorted to brutal ordeals to determine guilt or innocence.

sheriffs and the work of the hundred court was carried out by the manor court or court leet. Every year certain manor officers were chosen including the constable, ale-taster and bread-weigher. The post of constable was the most important of these as he helped the lord of the manor uphold the King's peace. It was his unpaid duty to combine his full-time employment with his police role, the tasks including reporting villagers' behaviour to the courts, arresting criminals until they were tried and calling out the hue and cry. The earliest record of a peace officer in the GMP area refers in 1252 to the existence of the petty constable of Rochdale.

The year 1285 saw the introduction of the Statute of Winchester which, amongst other things, laid down rules about town watchmen whose duty it was to report to the constable and to "watch the town continually all night, from the sun-setting to the sun-rising" when the city gates were shut. Should any suspicious strangers enter the town, the watchmen could hand them to the constable to be taken to court the following morning.

The Justice of the Peace Act 1361 was the next major stepping stone and this provided that each County in England be eligible to appoint up to four Justices of the Peace ". . . to restrain offenders and rioters and to arrest, take and chastise them according to the law and customs of the realm . ." The forerunners of today's magistrates, the JP's, could issue warrants to be executed by the constable but, like constables, they too were unpaid.

10. *top left:* A typical petty constable.

11. *bottom:* The parish constable carrying out his duties with staff, lantern and alarm bell.

Evolution of a Policing System

In the years leading up to the Tudor period, the feudal system dominated much of England and the barons and the Church were very rich and powerful. During the reigns of Henry VII (1485-1509) and Henry VIII (1509-1547) a major transition took place making the King the most powerful person in the land.

The majority of the population at that time still lived in the countryside and a system of Local Government developed under the control of the parish council and the Justices of the Peace. The parish council annually appointed various parish officers with specific community responsibilities. One such officer was the parish constable, often appointed by the town council in the larger cities, who would assist the Justices in upholding the peace. Two of the earliest parish constables in the Stretford area were Thomas Gilbody and Ralph Mosse who are known to have carried out duties in 1642. These officers were still unpaid and, apart from their wooden staff, did not wear an official uniform to denote their authority. In some areas the workload was becoming more and more onerous, and included carrying out some of the punishments and the constables' full-time employment was suffering. It was therefore decided in some areas to allocate funds to employ a paid 'beadle' or 'marshall' who would be provided with a uniform and official staff of office to greatly assist the parish constables in their work and Manchester had its own from 1614. Towards the end of the seventeenth century the constables could employ a deputy constable at a salary of £10 per annum.

12. The beadle was to remain a familiar part of the Manchester scene for the next 200 years.

Watchmen also continued to carry out their night duties but in 1663 the City of London began to employ paid watchmen, later becoming known as 'Charlies', carrying a bell, a lantern, a rattle and a staff to undertake this task. However, the low pay attracted only the old and frail or those who could not obtain alternative employment and was therefore not a very effective deterrent.

The seventeenth century saw the birth of the Agricultural Revolution and the slow beginnings of the Industrial Revolution which were to change the face of the country and its people forever.

The Old Look

The transition from England being mainly an agricultural society to becoming so industrialised that it became known as 'The workshop of the world' was a slow and painful one leading to traumatic upheaval and change for many of its inhabitants. The movement of so many people into inadequate English towns looking for work in the new industries led to social, economic and environmental problems never before experienced.

Although London was by far the worst affected by this transition, Manchester and other large cities witnessed terrible disorder leading to a lawless and brutal existence for many people. The shortage of housing meant inhabitants living cramped in decaying slums; sanitation was poor and disease rife; food and clothing were scarce commodities for those with little work and poverty, drunkenness and neglect were common. This in turn manifested itself in an increase in the level of crime and corruption.

13. Although Hogarth produced this famous work to illustrate the dangers of drinking gin as opposed to 'beneficial' beer drinking, it still imparts a dramatic picture of the degradation which was commonplace.

14. The high death toll in the Gordon Riots left a vivid impression on contemporary society but staunch die-hards still successfully opposed the idea of a professional police force.

This was the era when highwaymen attacked and robbed road travellers and the streets were swarming with thieves, footpads and pickpockets. When, as Horace Walpole described it in 1752, "... one is forced to travel, even at noon, as if one were going to battle..." it was becoming clear something would have to be done to alleviate the situation and London's answer to their own parcitular crime-wave was the introduction of the 'Bow Street Runners'. With the aid of a Government grant, it was possible to recruit six householders to serve as constables for more than the usual term of one year. They did not wear a uniform, although they did carry cutlasses and pistols, and they were paid a salary so they could devote themselves to their police duties full-time. Apart from a limited amount of success breaking up criminal gangs, they also had asistance from the public who gave them information about published news on crimes and criminals. By the end of the eighteenth century they had risen to about seventy in number.

In 1763 a small night horse patrol to guard roads leading into London was organised but this was short-lived due to the withdrawal of Government grant. It was reinstated in 1805 as the Bow Street horse patrol whose chief task was to rid the roads of highwaymen. Armed with cutlasses, pistols and truncheons, they were so well-organised that they were sometimes sent on commissions to other parts of the country and even abroad.

However, the year 1780 saw the Gordon Riots in London caused by the repeal of some antiquated anti-Catholic laws. The riots raged for almost a week and, as no peace-keeping force existed, the troops were finally called in, inciting the crowds even more and resulting in the deaths of 700 people and enormous damage to property. This led to the Government and London people thinking more seriously about ways of keeping the peace but none of the proposals was acceptable although they did introduce the River Police in 1800. This consisted of a sixty-strong paid team whose job it was to ensure the security of the rich cargo laid-up along the Thames. Their success was phenomenal and they became the largest professional police force in London, later forming part of the Metropolitan Police.

In Manchester the 1792 Manchester and Salford Police Act established a joint committee to form armed mounted night patrols in both cities with paid beadles to watch streets during the day but there is little evidence of these night patrols ever existing.

Also in 1792 the night watchmen of the Manchester township, who were employed by a separate body known as the Manchester Police and Improvement Commissioners, had their power extended not only to watch the streets but to light, cleanse and regulate them as well. In turn the adjoining townships of Hulme, Chorlton-on-Medlock, Ardwick and Cheetham, later becoming part of the City of Manchester, each had their own annually-elected constables and most had night watchmen.

The early part of the nineteenth century was overshadowed by the Napoleonic Wars with France. After 1815 many thousands of soldiers returned to their homes in search of jobs and housing but in many cases were met with unemployment and food scarcity.

Like many parts of the country, Manchester and its surrounding areas was affected by these post-war problems which in turn gave way to rioting and social upheaval. Industrial mechanisation was blamed and sabotage took place in the form of the Plug and Luddite Riots as attempts were made to wreck the factories housing new machinery which were seen as the cause of job losses.

15. A peaceful meeting about political reform held in Manchester's Petersfield ended in the killing of men, women and children by untrained yeomanry, whose heavy-handed tactics led to panic amongst the crowd. This took place on what is now the site of the Free Trade Hall near to St Peter's Square.

Riots broke out throughout the industrial areas of the Midlands and the North West, necessitating the employment of the Army to quell those which were most serious. Riots connected with electoral reform broke out in Manchester, the most famous being the Peterloo Massacre of August 1819 in which eleven people were killed and 600 were maimed or injured out of a 60,000 crowd.

Irrespective of this carnage the Government did little or nothing about law and order apart from introduce stricter laws to prevent large meetings such as this, and the local militia became the mainstays who dealt with such outbreaks. There was criticism that they often exerted too much violence but to many people they were preferable to a police force which could be used by the Government as tyrannical bullies and *agents provocateurs*. There was, however, some progress in the City of London and by 1828 a 450-strong force existed comprising the River Police, Bow Street horse and foot patrols and nine police officers plus around 4,500 watchmen known as 'proper Charlies'. This force did not reorganise until 1839.

It was not until 1822 when Sir Robert Peel from Bury became Home Secretary that real progress was made and the continuing breakdown of law and order was properly regulated. Peel was a skilful politician who tackled the problem cautiously in order to quell peoples' fears about the formation of a police force. His 'Bill for Improving the Police in and near the Metropolis' led in 1829 to the formation of the Metropolitan Police Act which provided a single police force for an area with a radius of seven miles from the centre of London.

16. Sir Robert Peel (1788-1850), founder of the modern police service.

The New Look

Peel's philosophy behind the introduction of the Metropolitan Police was that it was better to adopt a policy of crime prevention than to punish offenders after the crime had been committed. He also believed that by adopting a civilian-type uniform it would allay people's fears of the new police being a para-military organisation. He therefore decided that the uniform would comprise a frock-coat with stand-up collar on which would be fixed the constable's number, a wide leather belt and a tall hat with a thick leather top. A truncheon was carried together with a rattle to raise the alarm if help was required although this was augmented by a lantern for night duty.

As is the case today, officers had to work their way up through the ranks for promotion starting off as constable and only those capable would succeed. Chief Constables, however, tended to be appointed from the ranks of the military at this time.

The Metropolitan area was divided into seventeen Divisions each under a superintendent with teams of inspectors and sergeants in charge of the constables. Commissioners were appointed to oversee the new force and headquarters were in Whitehall Place in Westminster backing on to Scotland Yard — hence the modern name of the building. Over 3,000 men were recruited and entry was strictly regulated.

Applicants had to be under thirty-five years of age, in good health and strong, at least 5ft 7ins tall, able to read, write and have a good character reference.

The new police, or 'Peelers' as they became known, were very well-organised and highly-disciplined. At first they were met with much public hostility. Indeed a police officer was murdered by a mob at London's Cold Bath Fields in 1833 and a medal was struck privately to mark a blow against 'tyranny'. The parishes in particular objected to the greatly-increased costs of the new organisation, but eventually the new police became accepted and respected at home and abroad.

Parts of the country were still operating on a very ad hoc voluntary basis with unrest spreading rapidly. When outbreaks of violence occurred the local authorities called for the Army but their military methods incensed the rioters even more.

The situation in Manchester by the 1820s was that the day police were paid out of the poor rate and what little detective work was done was carried out with the aid of

18. The Cold Bath Field riots marked a low point in public feeling towards the new Peelers.

19. *below:* A rare glimpse of an 'old police' officer — a Manchester lock-up keeper.

17. The Peelers' outfit was designed to resemble these contemporary styles of men's fashion in order to prevent confusion with military uniform.

paid informers. The keepers of the local streeet lock-ups in the town carried out some of the investigations once a crime had been committed as well as acting as gaolers. By 1829 the deputy constable had under his command four beadles, seven assistants and four street keepers, reinforced on occasion by 200 Special Constables.

Due to the shining example of the Metropolitan Police other towns and cities were able to see how effective a police force could be. Crime was being cleared from the streets and many criminals were leaving London for other areas which had more haphazard ways of dealing with crime. Something had to be done even though it was realised that a police force based on the Metropolitan Police would be expensive and people were unwilling to contribute towards this extra cost.

Finally, in 1835 the Government passed the Municipal Corporations Act which was to change the policing methods of towns and boroughs throughout the country. Each town and borough was to be called a Corporation and each had to set up a police force which could be based on the London model or a system of their own. Many local authorities were reluctant to adopt the new methods because of the cost and by 1838 only half the boroughs in England and Wales had a police force. Many of the County areas outside the cities and towns fared even worse for, despite the County Police Act 1839, it was many years before they introduced a police force to their area.

The City of Manchester had its own problems in the setting-up of its Corporation and it was because of agitation by people such as Richard Cobden and William Neild that the Borough of Manchester was Incorporated on 23 October 1838. This lead to the Manchester Council appointing a Watch Committee in January 1839 to formulate a new borough police force, although this was initially beset by problems (see 'Manchester — A-E Divisions').

Similarly, although a slow process, other police forces, now within the area which makes up Greater Manchester Police started to become Incorporated under their own Borough Charters with Wigan in 1836 leading the way.

By the mid-1850s there were still thirteen boroughs and half the Counties of England without police forces so the Government stepped in and ordered these areas to adopt them. To enable this to take place the Government agreed to pay a quarter of the cost but only if these forces were run efficiently and Inspectors were appointed to visit every force to see if they came up to standard.

The take-up of the Government grant was in the beginning slow with only seven of the fifty-nine County forces being good enough to qualify. Some of the medium-sized boroughs took even longer but the larger towns reorganised quickly and very well.

According to the first Inspector's Report of September 1857 there were 237 forces in England and Wales and, though not all were satisfactory, some of the large towns, including Manchester and one or two Counties, were praised.

New police forces continued to be formed throughout the nineteenth century. Hyde, now part of the Greater Manchester area, was the last one to be formed in 1899.

The following pages briefly trace the historical highlights of the areas that were amalgamated into Greater Manchester Police on 1 April 1974 which now form the force's fourteen territorial Divisions.

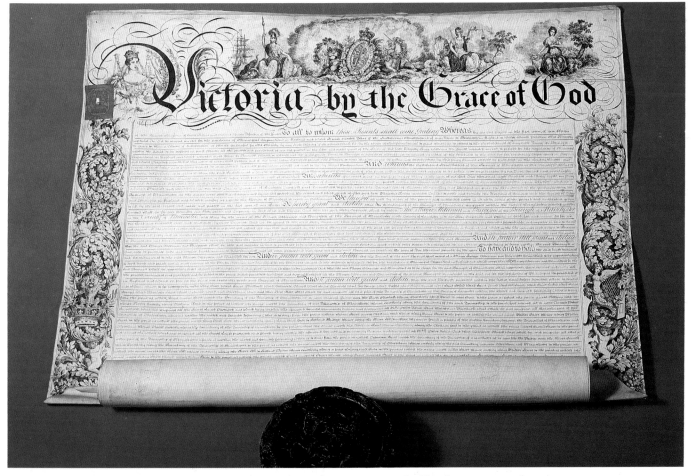

20. The 1838 Charter of Incorporation for Manchester.

Leaders of Men

Captain Edward Willis, 1842-1857.

William Henry Palin,
Chief Constable, 1857-1880.

Mr Charles Malcolm Wood, 1881-1896.
**Mr W Fell-Smith was the Acting
Chief Constable, 1897-1898.**

Sir Robert Peacock, 1898-1926.

Sir John Maxwell, 1926-1942.

Mr Joseph Bell, 1943-1958.

Sir John Andrew McKay, 1958-1966.

Mr William James Richards, 1966-1976.

Mr Cyril James Anderton, 1976-

The New Police - Policing from 1839

CENTRAL MANCHESTER — 'A' - 'E' Divisions

The first Watch Committee in Manchester was set up in January 1839 with the purpose of introducing a new borough force to the area but the court leet and police Commissioners refused to disband the old day police and night watchmen. They refused to recognise the new Watch Committee and barred them from police premises. The result was chaos with three distinct police bodies, totalling around six hundred men, operating at the same time in the town.

The threat of disturbance in the town by Chartists, the radical reform group, coupled with the disorganised state of the police, caused the Government to pass the Manchester Police Act of 1839 and appoint Sir Charles Shaw as Commissioner of a new police force run on the Metropolitan pattern. This came into being on 17 October 1839 with a strength of two hundred constables. Very soon afterwards the force was increased in size to 357 officers.

Shaw was later to go and establish a similar force in Bolton, again because of local disputes over Incorporation. Eventually problems regarding Incorporation were solved and the Manchester Borough Council gave a pledge to adopt the Government force but they would not accept control by Shaw. To overcome this problem the Commissioner's role was ended in September 1842 and on 24 October 1842

Captain Edward Willis was appointed Chief Constable at a salary of £450 with £50 allowance for expenses, commanding a force of sixty-five officers and 251 constables. The headquarters of the new force was in the old town hall building with an entrance in Cross Street.

22. The old Manchester Town Hall in which the new borough police established an office on Cross Street.

23. Manchester police officers parading-on for duty in the uniform worn between 1845 and 1865.

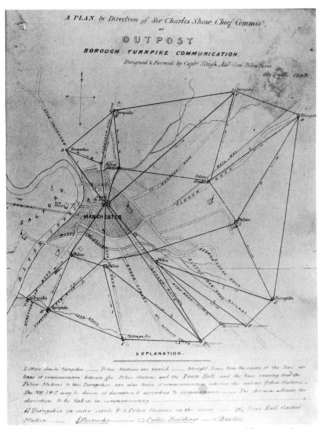

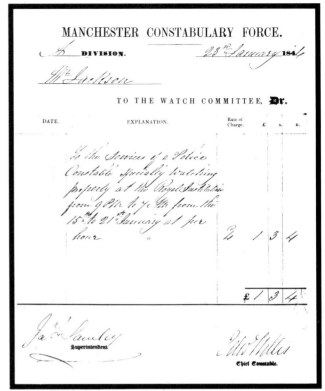

24. This map was prepared for Commissioner Shaw and was designed to show lines of communication between the town hall, police stations and the turnpikes on the town boundaries.

27. *above:* 4d . . . the cost of hiring a policeman to watch the Royal Institution in 1846.

25. *below:* Sergeant Charles Brett, the first Manchester police officer to be killed on duty — he was shot dead as supporters of the Fenian movement rescued two of their leaders from the prison van in which Brett was the escort officer. The subsequent trial and hanging of the men held responsible for his death began a controversy which lives on today.

26. *above:* Attack on the prison van escorted by Sergeant Brett.

28. The new Manchester Town Hall with its modified entrance on Lloyd Street to allow easier access for the 'Black Maria'.

1848 — A series of mass meetings and demonstrations were held in Manchester by the Chartists. Their demands included the right of every man to vote and the use of the secret ballot. By April of that year the authorities were afraid of a Chartist uprising so they reacted by swearing-in 12,000 Special Constables. On 10 April thousands of marchers set off for Manchester from surrounding areas but the town was garrisoned in preparation. As the marchers approached the city, the police warned them of the danger in proceeding and persuaded them to disperse. The new police had faced its first major incident and had succeeded in controlling the situation without the use of violence or military help.

1867 — The first Manchester policeman was murdered on duty. Two members of the Irish Nationalist group known as the 'Fenian Brotherhood' had been captured in the city. On 18 September Sergeant Charles Brett was escorting three prisoners to Belle Vue Prison in Hyde Road, Manchester, when the van in which he was travelling was attacked and the prisoners rescued. Brett was shot dead; the three men hanged for his murder became known as 'Manchester Martyrs'.

1868 — Jerome Caminada joined Manchester City Police at the age of twenty-four. He was later to become one of the greatest detectives ever to serve in the Manchester area. (See 'A Genius Amongst Detectives').

1877 — The present town hall in Albert Square was opened. The basement housed a police charge office and cells with admittance being gained from the Lloyd Street entrance.

1898 — Robert Peacock was appointed Chief Constable and introduced great policing changes — for example each policeman should have a definite meal time allotted during which he could eat his food at some convenient station. By 1911 most of the officers could take a twenty-minute meal break.

1908 —The taking of one day off in seven was authorised and special evening classes for police officers were introduced.

1928 — A new police box system was introduced involving the closing of old police stations and their replacement by a number of wooden huts or 'boxes'. Being unmanned, these boxes would release officers previously

29-30. *above left:* A well-earned rest! One day off in seven.
above right: One of the first Manchester 'phone boxes — this one was on the corner of Oldham Road and Thompson Street in the New Cross area.

31. A typical police canteen and rest-room in which limited cooking facilities comprising a tea-urn, a large frying pan and gas rings were available for officers' use.

employed on station duties and return them to the beat. The boxes contained a telephone which could be used by police or public. Whilst not replacing the police stations, the boxes remained a vital part of the communications network until the 1960s.

1933 — In June a drama and tragedy occurred at the Victoria Bridge over the River Irwell. A man named William Burke fell into the river and PC Tom Jewes went in to rescue him. Both were drowned. Jewes' funeral procession brought the city to a stand-still as 20,000 people lined the route.

1937 — Manchester City Police took control of their

Royal Humane Society.
INSTITUTED 1774.
Supported by Voluntary Contributions.
PATRON,
His Majesty the King
VICE PATRON,
H.R.H. the Duke of Connaught, K.G., &c.
PRESIDENT,
H.R.H. the Prince of Wales, K.G. &c.

At a Meeting of the Committee of the Royal Humane Society held at WATERGATE HOUSE, YORK BUILDINGS, ADELPHI, W.C.2. on the 15th day of August 1933

Present Admiral Cresswell J Eyres, D.S.C. Treasurer in the Chair

It was Resolved Unanimously

That the gallantry displayed by the late Police Constable Tom W. Jewes, who lost his life when attempting to save William Burke from drowning in the River Irwell at Manchester on the 10th June 1933 merits the highest praise of this meeting and the Committee in sympathizing with his relatives, desire to record their appreciation by the grant of the Honorary Testimonial of this Society inscribed on Vellum.

Edward
President.

Secretary.   Chairman.

32a-c. PC Tom Williamson Jewes who served between 1930 and his death in 1933. His posthumous Royal Society Award was signed by Edward, Prince of Wales, later Edward VIII.

new headquarters at Southmill Street. The Chief Constable stated "The new building made it possible to completely centralise administrative control and permitted the creation of several new departments in the scientific aspects of criminal investigation." For the first time special offices and laboratories were available for fingerprint work, photography and forensic examinations.

1939 — On 16 January a bomb exploded below the pavement in Hilton Street, Manchester. One man on his way to work in Smithfield Market was fatally injured. Two more pedestrians received serious injuries following explosions at Mosley Street and Princess Street. The bombs had been placed by members of the Irish Republican Army. Within twenty-four hours the police had arrested ten people after raids on their houses, recovering six barrels of explosives and forty sticks of gelignite. One of those arrested was sentenced to seven years' imprisonment.

1945 — In June the 'King of Forgers' — Herbert Winstanley — was caught passing forged pound notes whilst placing a bet at the Albion Stadium in Salford. At his home in Lindum Street, Rusholme, police found a complete forger's workshop and thousands of forged pound notes stacked in bundles. He received ten years' imprisonment.

1950s — This period saw the commencement of many experiments with radio vans and personal radio sets for beat officers. First tried and tested in the neighbouring Lancashire County force, the unit beat system or 'panda' system, with the twin features of the 'panda' patrol car and the personal radio, was introduced to Manchester in 1967. The officer in the car was to provide back-up to the area constables. Each district was divided into beats which became the responsibility of one individual constable who was free to police his beat with a certain amount of discretion.

1968 — On 1 April Manchester City Police amalgamated with the Salford City force to become Manchester and Salford Police force, Salford forming the 'F' Division of the 2,193-strong force.

1974 — With the creation of Greater Manchester Police, the old Manchester City area became the five central A — E Divisions of the new force, the Divisional headquarters of which to be based at:-

A — Manchester City Centre (Bootle Street)
B — Collyhurst (Rochdale Road)
C — Bradford (Grey Mare Lane)
D — Longsight (Stockport Road)
E — Rusholme (Platt Lane).

33. Still the headquarters of the central Manchester Division, the layout recognised the growing importance of science in police work.

34a. View of the damage caused by an explosion at the junction of Princess Street and Whitworth Street, 16 January 1939.

34b. The aftermath of the fatal explosion in Hilton Street near the present Greater Manchester Police Museum.

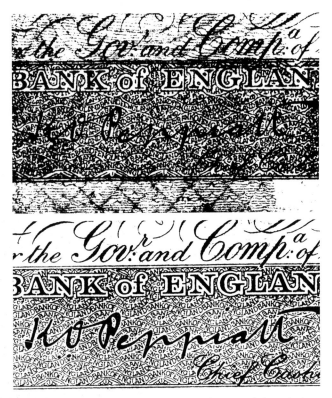

35a-d. Winstanley (*below*) — the master forger and the printing press he used (*top right*). Note the similarities between the genuine pound note and the fake (*top*).

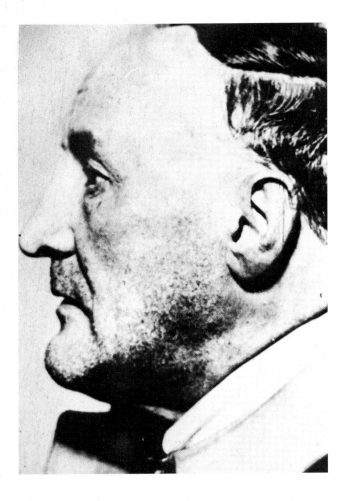

36. The Morris radio van was a commonplace sight in the streets of Manchester from the 1950s. The former radio vans used Morse code only.

37. An officer from Mill Street police station returning an escaped sheep to the Bradford Abattoir in the 1950s.

JEROME CAMINADA: A GENIUS AMONGST DETECTIVES

In his day, Jerome Caminada was extremely well-known and probably the most successful detective Victorian Manchester ever produced.

He was born in 1844 in Manchester's Deansgate of humble Irish-Italian parents. He left school to serve as an apprentice engineer with Mather & Platt's in Salford. He did not stay with them long and in 1868, when he was 24, joined Manchester City Police as a constable.

It is worth remembering that at the time Caminada joined the police Manchester was a very different place to now. In 1870 there were around 350,000 people living within the very small area of Cheetham to Deansgate, most of whom lived in abject poverty and slum conditions with squalid housing and poor sanitation. The death rate was very high, especially amongst children; cholera, typhoid and whooping cough being the major causes of death.

There was also terrible unemployment so, with no jobs and no money, many people turned to crime. In 1874 there were over 20,000 arrests made by a force of less than 800 men and, of those 20,000, around 19,000 of them could barely read or write. The worst areas were Ancoats and the ill-named Angel Meadow. Caminada himself wrote in his memoirs: "This district is deeply stained with drunkenness, debauchery, crime and vice in every shape . . . it was a foolish policeman indeed that entered Angel Meadow on his own." The commonest offences at this time were drunkenness, larceny, vagrancy and prostitution.

So it was to this world that Caminada entered as a policeman on a cold February night in 1868. That very night he was called to a woman nicknamed 'Fat Martha' who had been stabbed and thrown out on to the street. She was drunk and Caminada and three other officers spent the night carrying her around on a stretcher until she was sober.

His first conviction was against a man called Quinn in March 1868. Quinn, who owned a beerhouse, accused Caminada of being lazy and punched him on the nose. After a chase Caminada lost him but he had no sooner turned round to go back to his beat when Quinn reappeared and hit him round the ear and, during the ensuing struggle, he also bit Caminada's hand. He was eventually arrested and taken to the police station. Quinn was fined 10s 6d (52p) with 5s (25p) costs for assaulting a policeman.

After a series of successful arrests, Caminada was moved to the Detective Department which eventually became the CID. He was promoted to sergeant in 1871 and in 1888 was made an inspector.

Caminada's thirty-year career brought him into contact with every conceivable type of criminal, from the juvenile pickpocket to the Army officer who tried to sell State secrets to a foreign power. There were the amusing cases such as when he hid in a piano box to catch a thief at the Free Trade Hall or when he posed as a patient in order to expose 'quack' doctors.

There were also the serious cases, one of the most infamous becoming known as the 'Manchester Cab Murder'. In February 1889 a man called John Fletcher was drugged in a pub called The Three Arrows by a young man named Charles Parton. The two men left the pub and got into a Hansom cab where Parton robbed the apparently 'drunk' Fletcher. Parton then leapt out of the moving cab and left Fletcher to his fate. Parton however had been seen; the cab was stopped and Fletcher was found to be dead. Caminada was called in but he had very little information to go on. To begin with he did not know whether or not Fletcher had died a natural death. At this time there were very few scientific

38a. Jerome Caminada (1844-1914) — from apprentice engineer to the nationally-known head of detectives in Manchester. His determination and ingenuity made him feared by the underworld, whilst his autobiography highlights his passionate concern for prison reform and the underprivileged of the city.

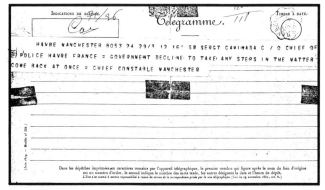

38b. Telegram recalling Caminada back to Manchester after his French pursuit.

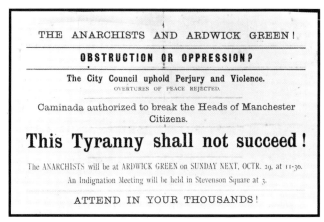

THE ANARCHISTS AND ARDWICK GREEN!

OBSTRUCTION OR OPPRESSION?

The City Council uphold Perjury and Violence.
OVERTURES OF PEACE REJECTED.

Caminada authorized to break the Heads of Manchester Citizens.

This Tyranny shall not succeed!

The ANARCHISTS will be at ARDWICK GREEN on SUNDAY NEXT, OCTR. 29, at 11·30.

An Indignation Meeting will be held in Stevenson Square at 3.

ATTEND IN YOUR THOUSANDS!

MUNICIPAL ELECTION, 1907.

OPENSHAW WARD.

VOTE FOR CAMINADA,

THE PRACTICAL MAN.

Your Friend and Neighbour.

VOTE FOR CAMINADA

The Strong Opponent of Atheism and disastrous Socialism.

VOTE FOR CAMINADA

The old Trade Unionist,
who is so thoroughly conversant with
Openshaw and Manchester.

The Candidature of

Mr. JEROME CAMINADA

is heartily approved of by the

Manchester Ratepayers' Association.

aids to determine the cause of death and there were no Home Office pathologists. Caminada sent some of Fletcher's organs for tests and it was eventually revealed that he had been poisoned.

Caminada set out to find the murderer with only a vague description and his detective instincts to go on. The trail led to Parton, and Caminada found property belonging to the dead man in Parton's home. He was arrested and charged with murder.

At his trial Parton claimed he only drugged Fletcher so he could rob him, and admitted to having used this trick previously on other men. He was however found guilty of murder and sentenced to death although this was later commuted to life imprisonment. The significance of this case is that it took Caminada only twenty-one days from the time of death to find the murderer, find the evidence, have Parton committed for trial, tried and convicted.

Another interesting case concerned one Robert Horridge who, over a period of about twenty years, was repeatedly arrested by Caminada. Horridge was in trouble with the law from an early age. At the age of thirteen he was sent to prison for six months for stealing money. Caminada first met Horridge in 1869 when he was searching his house for stolen property. Horridge evaded capture for many years but he was finally caught in 1881 and sent to Dartmoor. However he managed to escape and was shot three times before he was recaptured. Only a few weeks after his release in 1887 he was seen by a policeman trying to break into a shop in Rochdale Road. Constables Parkin and Bannon gave chase but he shot and wounded them with a revolver.

Horridge had acquired the revolver for the specific purpose of shooting Caminada if he should try arresting him again. Caminada said on hearing this information: "This certainly was very pleasant news but, knowing the desperate character of the man, I was not surprised to hear it". Caminada and his men, disguised as labourers, traced Horridge to Liverpool. At 10.30 pm one night Caminada saw his quarry in Duke Street. He seized him and said "Hello Bob, how are you?" Horridge tried to get to his gun but Caminada had come prepared and says in his memoirs: "I drew my revolver and, placing the muzzle to his mouth with the weapon at full cock, said: "If there is any nonsense with you, you'll get the contents of this." Horridge went quietly at first but later tried to escape yet again. Caminada drew his gun, but to use his own words: "I wasn't going to waste a bullet on him" and so he beat him over the head with the butt of his revolver. Horridge appeared at the Manchester Assizes on 27 November 1887 and was sentenced to penal servitude for life. He never bothered Caminada again.

Caminada was also indirectly involved with the Fenians. In 1881 he pursued across France two men who were suspected of causing explosions in London. In 1882 he shadowed all over America and Ireland the man who had killed both the Chief Secretary of Ireland, Lord Frederick Cavendish, and Mr T H Burke in Phoenix Park, Dublin.

Throughout his successful career Caminada was responsible for the imprisonment of 1,225 people. In 1882 there were 2,530 beerhouses and 524 public houses as well as the illegal drinking dens and stills. Caminada closed 400 of these places for serving poor-quality drinks or for lewd behaviour.

During the last century policemen were sometimes given financial rewards for successful cases and Caminada

38c-e. In 1907 Caminada began a second career in local politics. His previous police experience led him to propose political change in the organisation of the force, its stations and manpower.

was no exception. He received many rewards, his largest being £500 (nearly two years' salary) for catching a gang of forgers.

Caminada once went to court to solve a dispute over who should get a particular reward, himself or a man called Pingstone. The court resolved that the reward should be divided between them. However £100 would not have covered Caminada's court expenses so a committee of Manchester citizens was formed and they raised £300 by subscription for him. Caminada also once said he had been praised by the Watch Committee over 1,200 times.

In December 1897 he became the first superintendent of the Manchester CID with a salary of £325 a year (the ordinary constable earned £1 6s (£1.30) a week). He eventually retired in March 1899 on a pension of £210 a year which the Watch Committee had raised from £195 10s 10d as a sign of gratitude for his services. They also presented him with an illuminated scroll.

For a time he worked as an estate agent and a private detective but he always kept in touch with what was happening in the Manchester police force. He was very critical of police administration and opposed many council schemes. He joined local politics and became a councillor for Openshaw in 1907 and was narrowly defeated in the local elections of 1910. He was very outspoken and made a lot of political enemies.

In 1913 Caminada was hurt in an accident in North Wales when a charabanc (a type of bus) overturned. He never really recovered from his injuries and died at his home in Moss Side in March 1914 aged seventy. He is buried in Manchester's Southern Cemetery.

What was the man really like? He made a stern enemy but his many acts of kindness were never forgotten and he was a loyal friend. He also befriended many of the people he had had imprisoned and if they came to him for help or financial aid he never refused them. He was very outspoken but was always ready to back up his opinions. He could be very humorous and, as one reads his memoirs, one senses he thought everything a bit of a 'lark' but underneath he was deadly serious. He had boundless energy and confidence in what he did.

Perhaps one should remember that first and foremost Caminada was a policeman — and a very good one. When he died fifteen years after he had retired, his death made national headlines and tributes poured in from all over the country.

SALFORD

'F' Division

Following the 1792 Manchester and Salford Police Act the Commissioners for Salford decided to divide the area into seven districts and employ fourteen watchmen. A deputy constable and a number of beadles were to act as day police.

1833 — The day police were reorganised to comprise a superintendent who received £140 a year, two beadles, an assistant beadle and a police clerk.

1835 — The Municipal Corporations Act enabled nearby Manchester to become an Incorporated Borough and establish its own professional police force. However, Salford did not apply for Incorporation at first, wishing to maintain the old system of law and order, but when it became clear

that Salford would be policed by the new Lancashire Constabulary, rather than by local officers, Salford decided to form its own force and was granted a Charter of Incorporation on 16 April 1844. The new force consisted of a Chief Constable, a superintendent, four inspectors, a clerk, twenty-seven policemen and six supernumeries. John Diggles was appointed the first Chief Constable.

1845 — It was alleged that the Chief Constable and superintendent had been claiming sums of money, paying the police officers a portion of it, and pocketing the difference. The Watch Committee considered the charges and dismissed both officers from the force.

The new Chief Constable was Edwin Sheppard but he was to resign in disgust two years later after what he described as "two years of continued annoyance" at the Watch Committee's interference in the work of the Chief Constable.

His successor, Mr Stephen Neal, was to fare little better. After being fined by the Watch Committee for his handling of a case, in 1852 he was dismissed. In his defence the Chief Constable issued a pamphlet entitled 'Despotic Tyranny' and commented that one particular member of the

39. An eighteenth century watch box possibly used by a member of the night patrols which were established by the Manchester and Salford Police Act of 1792.

40. Police in Salford providing clothing for poor and crippled children in August 1923.

41. Salford City police officers circa 1900.

Chief Constables of the

Salford City Police Force

JOHN DIGGLES, Esq.,
1844—1845.

CAPTAIN E. SHEPHERD,
1845—1848.

STEPHEN NEALE, Esq.,
1848—1852.

JAMES TAYLOR, Esq.,
1852—1866.

WILLIAM C. SYLVESTER,
Esq., 1866—1868.

EDWARD HIBBERT, Esq.,
1868—1869.

CAPTAIN R. W. TORRENS,
1869—1880.

WILLIAM L. MARSHALL,
Esq., 1880—1889.

COMMANDER C. T. SCOTT,
1889—1898.

JOHN W. HALLAM, Esq.,
1898—1908.

MAJOR C. V. GODFREY,
O.B.E., 1908.

MAJOR C. V. GODFREY, O.B.E.,
Chief Constable.
Photograph by Lafayette, Manchester.

42. Major Cedric V Godfrey, OBE, Chief Constable of Salford City Police from 1908-1946, surrounded by the names of his predecessors.

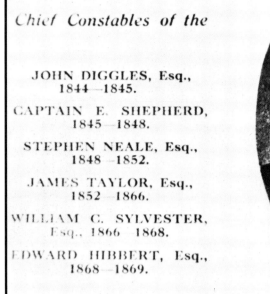

Take this home to your Parents

ELEMENTARY WING.

SALFORD CITY POLICE.

TO PARENTS AND OTHERS

A child was killed recently when he ran off the footpath into the road without first looking to the left and right, and at the Inquest the Coroner made the following remarks :—

"The Authorities take all precautions to prevent or reduce the number of accidents by the erection of street signs, safety islands and marked crossings, and lectures are also given in the schools by Teachers and competent Police Officers.

The children in the schools are instructed and continually warned of the dangers and the care which is always necessary when crossing a road. Unfortunately, of course, children under school age do not have the benefit of such instruction, neither do they understand the road signs nor the danger to which they are exposed when crossing a busy thoroughfare.

I personally feel that much can be done by parents of children of tender years if they will only take the trouble of CONTINUALLY and not casually, warning their children of the danger of crossing a road by themselves, and impressing upon their minds that they must not leave the footpath unless an adult is with them."

I earnestly agree with the remarks of the Coroner and would urge upon all that if accidents to children in the City are to continue to show a decline the Police must have the co-operation of every Citizen of Salford in helping the children when on or about the roads and streets of the City.

C. V. GODFREY, Major,
Chief Constable.

Chief Constable's Office,
Town Hall, Salford.
October 1st, 1935.

43a-c. Salford Police led the way in the teaching of road safety to children. Handouts such as these brought the message to every household. Major Godfrey also arranged for the showing of accident prevention films in Salford schools.

Committee, Mr Gendall, had persecuted himself and his predecessor, Sheppard.

1908 — Major Cedric Godfrey was appointed Chief Constable and served until 1946. He introduced motor vehicles, telephones and police telephone boxes to the city.

1920s — As a response to growing traffic problems and increasing death toll on the roads, Major Godfrey launched a major road-safety campaign. He showed safety films to 20,000 children in Salford and closed certain streets to traffic, thus creating safe play areas.

1933 — Lectures on road safety, given by Salford Police, began in schools and so successful was the campaign that between September 1935 and October 1936 not a single child was killed on Salford's roads.

1937 — Major Godfrey published his book *Road Sense for Children* and was regarded by many as a leading authority on road safety.

1940 — Salford bombed during the 'heavy blitz' of December and 197 people killed.

1945 — First policewomen appointed.

1968 — Salford City Police amalgamated with Manchester City Police.

1974 — On amalgamation, Salford became the 'F' Division of Greater Manchester Police.

44. *right:* Members of Salford City Police on their final parade before amalgamation with Manchester and Salford Police on 1 April 1968.

45. Police radio room in Salford Town Hall, 1956.

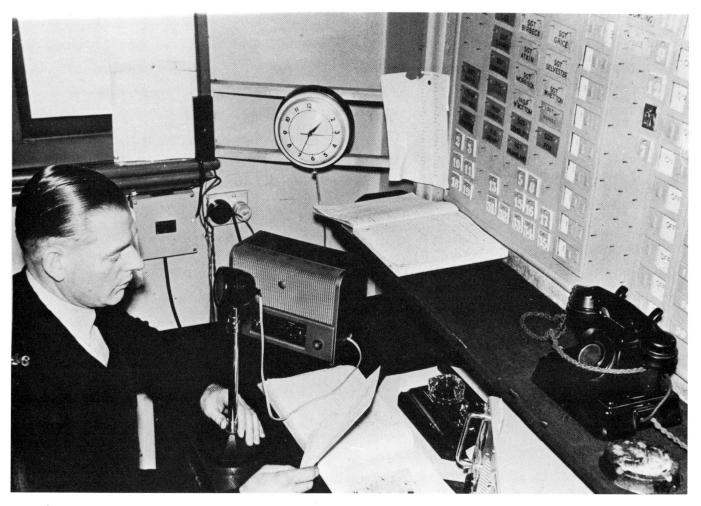

46. Members of Salford City Police band as actors in the 1953 film Hobson's Choice.

47. *below:* Salford detachment of officers boarding the London-bound train at Piccadilly Station on their way to perform duties on the route of Her Majesty Queen Elizabeth II's Coronation. Special 'Mutual Aid' helmets were worn instead of the usual Salford helmet to blend in with the Metropolitan Police.

TAMESIDE
'G' Division

Ashton-under-Lyne

The keeping of the peace in Ashton was largely carried out by locally-elected constables and deputy constables until 1848 when a professional police force of thirteen men was introduced.

The force was created at a particularly turbulent time in Ashton's history. The town had long been a centre of the Chartist Movement and a number of stormy meetings had been held in the Chartist Rooms. One such incident occurred in August 1848 when Police Constable James Bright of the Ashton force encountered a group of men causing trouble. He attempted to persuade the men to return home but instead was stabbed and shot dead on the corner of Stamford Street and Bentinck Street.

Despite this early set-back, the force was not deterred and continued to maintain law and order throughout the nineteenth century. Indeed the Chief Constable of Ashton in the 1860s was presented with a decorated truncheon for his skilful handling of the Cotton Riots in the town.

The early twentieth century saw the introduction of the police telephone box and pillar systems in Ashton. The boxes were wooden sheds containing a telephone while the pillars were merely a cast-iron pillar with a telephone box on top. Both police and public were able to make use of the new system.

1939 - The town was divided into eight beats, most of which used police boxes and pillars as the starting or finishing points instead of the central police stations. There were also four bicycle patrols in the town at this time.

After the Second World War, the force had grown in size to sixty-three officers but, in keeping with national policy, it was decided that such a small force should amalgamate with a larger neighbouring one and so on 1 April 1947 Ashton Borough Police became part of the Lancashire Constabulary.

Stalybridge

In the days prior to the creation of a professional police force in Stalybridge, a constable and a deputy constable kept the peace in the area.

Although Stalybridge appears to have later had two paid officers to act as constables, nothing much changed until 1857 when, in August, a professional full-time police force was introduced. The new force only had a strength of eleven men and morale was not high among the new officers.

In February 1862, William Chadwick joined the force as Chief Constable, having previously served as an inspector in the Ashton-under-Lyne Borough Police. He quickly improved the force's efficiency and was to remain Chief Constable until 1899.

1862 — In June Police Constable William Jump was murdered. Jump was a member of the neighbouring Lancashire force who had been assigned to help Stalybridge Police guard brick-makers' yards against sabotage by a rival group of workers. One night one such yard was attacked, Jump was shot dead and another officer, named Harrop, wounded. The shooting aroused much anger and the three men responsible were soon caught.

48. *top:* The Chief Constable of Ashton's decorated truncheon.

49. The beat books described the patrols in detail including the streets covered, the direction of working, the telephone boxes from where to make calls to Divisional headquarters and where to take meal breaks.

ASHTON-UNDER-LYNE
BOROUGH POLICE

WORKING
OF BEATS

J. Andrew & Co., Ltd. Printers, Ashton-under-Lyne

1866-1868 — Stalybridge witnessed the first in a series of 'Murphy Riots'. An Irishman named William Murphy, a Catholic who had seceded from his faith, went about the country holding meetings at which he strongly condemned the Catholic religion and particularly the priesthood. The first meeting in Stalybridge was held at the Peoples' Hall and ended in uproar. Fighting between Catholics and Protestants broke out and rioting began which lasted three days. Later a gang of about five-hundred hooligans arrived from Ashton and devastated Thomas Street. They were repelled by an inspector and seven armed officers. Murphy was eventually shot dead at a meeting.

1920s — Motorcycles were being used and by 1928 the

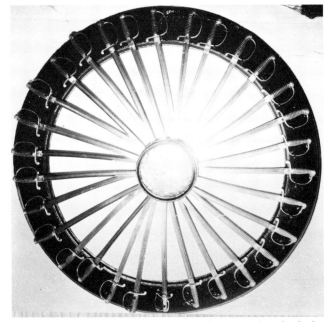

50. *left:* A Found Property slip. It is not known whether the finder of this roll of Danish bacon returned to collect it six months later!

51. *below:* Sergeant Thompson (first left) with Stalybridge mounted officers circa 1895.

52. *above:* Cutlasses purchased by Stalybridge Commissioners and Stalybridge Corporation between 1830 and 1863. They were last used in the Murphy Riots in 1866.

53. Photograph of William Chadwick from his autobiography "Reminiscences of a Chief Constable".

force had two motor cycle and side-car combinations and a strength of thirty officers.

By 1947 the force had increased in size to thirty-five but on 1 April 1947 the Stalybridge force merged with Cheshire Constabulary.

Hyde

The policing of the Hyde area was undertaken by the Cheshire County force until the end of the nineteenth century. The Chief Constables of Cheshire, in keeping with other areas up until the early twentieth century, were men with military backgrounds. For example Captain Arrowsmith, who was appointed superintendent of Hyde Division in 1871 and became Chief Constable in 1878, was a man who demonstrated his military background by deciding to run the police in Army tradition and style.

Captain Arrowsmith considered his superintendents to be mounted officers and were therefore required to wear spurs. Indeed superintendents, upon retirement, were replaced by ex-Army men so that a military character would be given to the force.

1881 — Hyde became a Municipal Borough. At this time it was still policed by the Cheshire force with a strength of one inspector, five sergeants and seventeen constables under the command of Superintendent E J Lingard.

1899 — On 1 April it became a separate police force with Mr W J A Danby as Chief Constable and an authorised establishment of one Chief Constable, two inspectors, seven sergeants and thirty constables. The residue of the old Hyde Division became the Dukinfield Division.

1947 — On 1 April Hyde merged again with the Cheshire County force and formed the north-east Division with Stalybridge and Dukinfield.

1974 - On amalgamation with Greater Manchester Police these areas formed part of the 'G' Division.

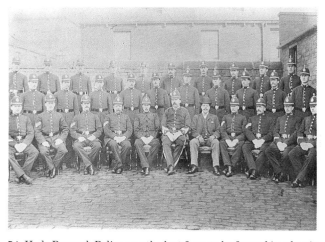

54. Hyde Borough Police was the last force to be formed in what is now the Greater Manchester Police area. It was also the shortest-lived — only 48 years separate this photograph taken on its first day from its merger with the Cheshire Constabulary force in 1947.

55. An Ashton Borough Police mobile patrol van in April 1944.

56. Three Hyde police officers prepare to celebrate the crowning of Edward VII.

STOCKPORT
'J' Division

During the Industrial Revolution Stockport became a very thriving industrial and business area but its economic boom incurred much unrest. The Luddite Movement led to serious riots and disruption and during the Blanketeers March through Stockport an innocent by-stander was killed by a soldier.

1842 — The Plug Riots occurred which involved workers smashing the plugs on mill boilers in protest at the 'new technology' being introduced.

1852 — Fighting broke out between Catholic and Protestant labourers following a Roman Catholic children's procession. This resulted in dreadful damage and over a hundred men were arrested by the Infantry.

1860 — The Stockport Police superintendent reported that 783 people had been arrested in that year, 310 of these being for drunkenness.

1870 — Stockport adopted a full-time police force and fifteen men were appointed under Chief Constable Lieutenant Blair Sharples. The uniform of the new force consisted of a dark-blue close-necked tunic with matching trousers and a 'Shako'-style peaked hat (a stiffened cloth peaked hat based on a nineteenth century Infantry helmet — See 'Uniforms, Helmets and Equipment'). By 1874 the force had grown to seventy-two officers and by 1901 had increased to 112.

1922 — Mr G W Rowbotham became Chief Constable. He introduced many innovations into the force including motor cycles and motor cars, Stockport becoming pioneers in police radio communications.

1929 — Stockport set up a police box system and eighteen boxes were installed in various locations in the town from which members of the public could use the boxes to telephone the emergency services.

1960s — Local Government structures came under review and it was felt that the changing methods of policing necessitated larger units of police force. One proposal was to merge with Manchester and Salford forces but this was discarded.

1967 — Stockport Borough together with Wallasey, Birkenhead, Chester City and the old Cheshire Police, became part of the new Cheshire Constabulary; the headquarters of the north-east Cheshire Division of this new force being based at Stockport.

On 4 June the same year one of the worst air disasters ever to occur in Great Britain happened in the centre of Stockport. It involved an Argonaut air-liner owned by British Midland Airways travelling from Palma (Majorca) to Manchester Airport. Of the eighty-four people on board, seventy-two died, twelve survived.

1968 — A special Detective Squad was set up to deal with the growing incidence of burglaries in the wealthy areas of the town.

1974 — Stockport became part of the 'J' Division on amalgamation into Greater Manchester Police.

57. The rapidly-expanding industrial towns of the North West were frequently the scene of rioting and disorder.

58. Caught in the act! A police officer arresting a whisky smuggler.

60. Most of the police boxes in the Stockport area were made of concrete and this one in Adswood Road, photographed in 1968, is a good example.

59. Stockport Borough Police in 1926.

61. A group of Stockport Borough police officers in Market Place circa 1920s. In many smaller forces borough pride was exemplified in the elaborate helmets worn by the officers — and Stockport was no exception!

62. Inspecting the wreckage of the Stockport air disaster in June 1967.

BOLTON
'K' Division

During the early part of the nineteenth century Bolton, in common with much of the country, suffered much social unrest due to protests by Luddites opposed to the use of new technology and Chartists who were seeking Parliamentary reforms. Whenever trouble broke out, Special Constables had to be sworn-in.

In 1838 Bolton was granted a Charter of Incorporation, the effect of which was to remove power from the self-elected town council and introduce a freely-elected town council. This new council was entitled to form a Watch Committee and maintain a police force but there was much opposition to it. A temporary police force was set up for a few months until November 1839 when the Bolton Borough Police force was formed under Superintendent Hyram Simpton. Forty men were initially sworn-in by a Government Commissioner. This body of men was to be a Government force although control of them was to be delegated to the town council. These men were very unpopular with the public.

1842 — Superintendent John Boyd became Chief of Police for Bolton Borough. He did not hold office long and was replaced by James Harris who introduced the use of paid informants.

1867 — James Harris resigned and was replaced by Thomas Beech commanding, by that time, a seventy-strong force. This was a violent period in Bolton's history and each constable was issued with a cutlass. In common with other towns in the north-west, Bolton was troubled by the activities of the 'Fenian Brotherhood' and 2,151 Special Constables were sworn in.

1868 — Bolton was considered by the Government to be adequately policed as it passed an inspection by the Government Inspector.

1877 — Mr Beech resigned and was replaced by John Holgate who was required by the Watch Committee to live close to the town hall. By this time the force had grown to 103 in number.

1898 — Astley Bridge, Breightmet, Darcy Lever and other townships were brought under Bolton. The force was increased in manpower to 166 and split into Divisions, the central Division being at the town hall.

1911 — Mr Fred Mullineaux from Liverpool became the Chief Constable. Working conditions of constables were improved. Notebooks for police officers were introduced for the first time and an administrative section was set up.

1912 — Walking sticks were introduced for inspectors and sergeants and it was the practise to carry the stick as a symbol of rank and to show that they were on duty.

1913 — King George V visited Bolton, the first by a reigning Monarch. The visit was a complete success and the police force was complimented on the way it handled the crowd.

1914-1918 — During the war there was a drain on manpower as many men were recalled to their former regiments and Bolton appointed Special Constables to provide cover.

1919 — A Womens' Branch was set up comprising of four policewomen. Although they were a success it is unlikely they were given the full powers and status of a police constable.

1925 — The force acquired their first motor car — a Daimler.

63. *top right:* John Holgate, Chief Constable of Bolton Borough Police from 1877-1911, who joined the force in 1858.

64. Members of the Policewomen's Department of Bolton Borough Police in 1923.

1930 — Mr W J Howard became Chief Constable.

1931 — A pedal cycle patrol was formed.

1939-1945 — During the Second World War, to provide emergency cover, Bolton relied on the Police War Reserve, the Women's Auxiliary Corps and four hundred Special Constables. In March 1945 King George VI and Queen Elizabeth visited Bolton.

1946 — On 9 March a major tragedy occurred at Burnden Park football ground in Bolton when a barrier collapsed killing thirty-three people and injuring five hundred more of the 65,419-strong crowd. It happened during the FA quarter-final between Bolton and Stoke City when a number of unauthorised spectators climbed into the embankment enclosure causing the barrier to break.

1957 — Mr Edward Barker from Lancashire Police College became Bolton's Chief Constable. During his time in office Bolton Police used four motor scooters in police work for a short period, which were later replaced by motor cars.

On 12 September mining subsidence in Fylde Street in Moses Gate led to the devastation of the entire area and the evacuation of four hundred people from their homes for over three months.

1961 — On 2 May a major fire swept through the Top Storey Club in Crown Street, Bolton. Nineteen people died, four as a result of jumping from the top floor window of the club to the River Croal forty feet below and four others were injured and taken to hospital. In the panic people with their clothes ablaze also flung themselves into the river where police with search-lights focused on the water were waiting to rescue them.

1962 — Radar introduced as a means of detecting speeding motorists.

1964 — Mr Barker resigned, to be replaced by Mr John William Moody, the last Chief Constable of Bolton.

1969 — After nearly 130 years of existence, Bolton Borough Police amalgamated with Lancashire Constabulary and became the 'K' Division of that force.

1973 — On 8 February Mohammed Shafiq became the first non-white police officer to join Lancashire Constabulary's Bolton Division. Born in Pakistan, PC Shafiq was promoted to sergeant in June 1980 and is still a serving police officer in GMP.

1974 — On the formation of Greater Manchester Police Bolton continued as 'K' Division of the new force.

65. King George VI and Queen Elizabeth, who visited Bolton Town Hall in March 1945, are accompanied by Mr Howard (Chief Constable) and Captain Hordern (Chief Constable of Lancashire).

66. PC (later Inspector) Norris with the first Bolton police motor car in 1925.

67. The aftermath of the Burnden Park football ground disaster in March 1946.

68-69. Clearing-up after the Fylde Street disaster which disrupted the lives of residents for many months.

70. Emergency services coping with the tragic fire at Bolton's Top Storey Club.

71. Mr J W Moody (1964-1969), Bolton's last Chief Constable.

72. PC Mohammed Shafiq, the first non-white police officer in the Greater Manchester area.

WIGAN
'L' Division

In 1662 Charles II stated that Wigan was designated an 'Ancient Borough' and it was granted "as a special token of our favour for its loyalty to us" the right to carry a sword before the Mayor as well as other rights and privileges. This was the governing charter of the town until the Municipal Corporations Act 1835.

With the introduction of industrialisation in the nineteenth century, Wigan, with its eight cotton mills, saw outbreaks of Luddite violence. A Wigan volunteer troop of light horsemen was raised to preserve order in the locality.

In 1835 the Municipal Corporations Act allowed boroughs to form Watch Committees and in 1836 the Wigan force was formed controlling an area of three and a half square miles.

The first meeting of the Watch Committee was held at the town hall in Market Place on 6 January 1836. The acting Chief Constable of Manchester suggested to the Wigan Watch Committee that a preventative police force of forty officers should be formed and they should provide a charge book, bail book, occurrence book and officers' time and conduct book. Hugh Fagan of Wigan was appointed as constable and goal-keeper at a salary of £1 5s 0d (£1.25) a week. John Whittle was appointed Chief Constable with a salary of £200 per annum. William Lancaster was made constable of Scholes. These three men comprised the day police and William Halliwell, Henry Bolton and Thomas Bradley were appointed night police. Therefore a total of six men were appointed but pay and conditions were poor. For example the day police were required to be on duty from eight o'clock in the morning until eleven o'clock at night, Sunday to Friday, and worked longer hours on the Saturday. All six were eventually to be sacked for breaches of discipline.

The uniform of the new police consisted of a brown coat with stand-up collar, brown waistcoat, grey trousers and a Peeler-style top-hat. Later the uniform was changed to the Liverpool pattern of light trousers and dark blue tail-coat with seven buttons, again with top-hat. In 1840 the Chief Constable, Mr Whittle, was sacked for drunkenness and replaced by Mr Thomas Latham.

Early 1880s — The force increased in size to over fifty men.

1883 — A total of 2,621 persons were taken before magistrates by the force.

1886 — The Chief Constable, Mr F T Webb, reported the only crime increasing was drunkenness. He also commented that the practise of displaying goods outside shops was an invitation to a "hungry or reckless person" to take them. He felt that if shop-keepers insisted on outside displays, they should not report any losses to the police.

1888 — Wigan became a County Borough and had a population of about 50,000.

1904 — Wigan Police took on the policing in the township of Pendleton.

1920s — Motorcycles were introduced for police patrol work.

1926 — During the year of the General Strike and Miners' Strike, police in the area were heavily stretched and, during one incident at Pemberton Colliery, police baton-charged a crowd, souring their relationship with the public for many years.

73. A typical open-air market of the kind which caused policing problems for the Wigan Chief Constable.

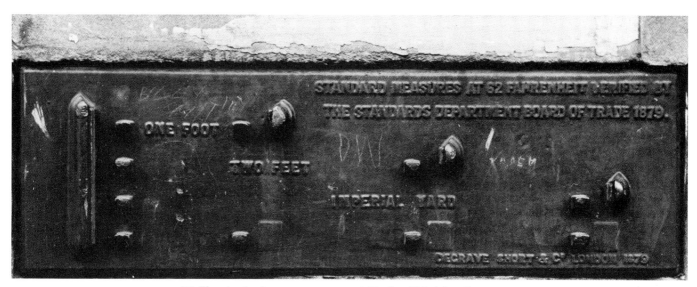

74. The standard measures gauge outside the old Leigh police station.

1930s — In the early part of the decade the police officer's salary was set at £3 5s 0d (£3.25) a week and remained at that level until 1945.

1958 — The force had risen to 147 officers, seven of which were women. During the same year one of the Wigan policewomen was highly commended for the courageous arrest of a man wanted for murder in St Helens.

1965 — Wigan established a dog section with three dogs and handlers.

1969 — After 130 years under the leadership of thirteen Chief Constables, Wigan joined Lancashire Constabulary to become 'H' Division.

1974 — Wigan changed from 'H' to 'L' Division in the new Greater Manchester Police amalgamation.

75. A group of Wigan Borough police officers outside the King Street headquarters in 1926.

76. One of the most onerous duties in the Wigan area was the policing of colliery disputes either as here during the 1912 Miners' Strike or later in the General Strike of 1926.

77. Chief Superintendent Davies of Lancashire County pointing out the expanded Wigan Division which would now include the old Wigan Borough area, following the 1969 amalgamation. Looking on are from left to right:Acting Chief Constable Bill Taylor, Inspector Norman Robinson, PC Dunn and Police Sergeant Croghan.

78. PC Lowe using a police pillar in 1957. Note the pocket-book stand protruding from the box.

79-80. One aspect of nineteenth century policing duty that is often overlooked is the social work carried out by different forces, ranging from soup kitchens organised by Superintendent Bent to the provision of clothing and shoes for needy children.

TRAFFORD
'M' Division

Stretford and Altrincham

In former centuries much of the Trafford area was open countryside and, despite the building of the Bridgewater Canal in 1761 which led to easier communications with Manchester, the area around the present-day Greater Manchester Police headquarters, called Throstle's Nest Wood, was known as a haunt of thieves. Indeed in November 1803, the *Manchester Mercury* reported that one Thomas Aldred of Urmston had been robbed of £800 and shot dead by highwaymen.

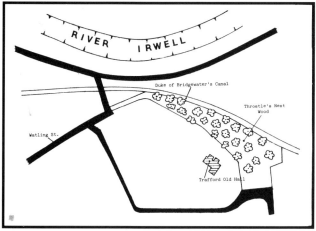

81. *above:* The quiet, leafy Throstle's Nest Wood area in 1819 — a far cry from the bustling junction of Chester Road and Talbot Road near to the site of the present-day force headquarters.

1839 — The Stretford area became part of the Manchester Division of the Lancashire Constabulary and for the first time Stretford had a professional police force. The officers wore the standard uniform of top-hat, blue tail coat and white or blue trousers.

Altrincham was part of Cheshire and remained so until 1974. Altrincham police wore the distinctive 'Shako-style' helmet of stiffened cloth-cap with a peak and neck-guard until the late 1920s, while forces in the neighbouring areas had long since changed to the familiar helmet that is worn today.

1868 — One of the most famous Commanders of the Manchester Division of Lancashire Constabulary was Superintendent James Bent. Born in Eccles in 1828, he was appointed head of the Manchester Division at Old Trafford and held the post until his death in 1901. Having served the force for over forty years, Mr Bent became very well-known in the area, not least for the large amount of social work he undertook in his spare time.

1876 — Much alarm was caused on the Division by the murder of a police officer in the course of his duty. PC Nicholas Cock was shot dead as he attempted to arrest an armed burglar who had just ransacked a house on Cock's beat. At first all the evidence pointed to two brothers called Habron. Bent had them arrested. At their trial they were found guilty of involvement in the death of PC Cock and one of them was sentenced to death but reprieved on account of his youth. However, there was a sensation when a notorious burglar and murderer, Charles Peace, many months later, confessed to the murder of PC Cock while awaiting execution for another murder. This confession was accepted and the Habron brothers were released and compensated for their prison ordeal.

1878 — Superintendent Bent decided to set up a soup kitchen for the poor and destitute at the drill hall of East

82. The impressive frontage of Henshaw's School for the Blind and the Royal Institute for the Deaf which were demolished to make way for the Chester House headquarters.

Union Street police station in Old Trafford. In the years 1888 and 1889 over 156,000 meals were served and by April 1891 nearly 1,600,000 people had received a meal at the police station. Many children also received clothing provided by a fund administered by the police.

1887 — In May the Royal Jubilee Exhibition was opened on Talbot Road, Old Trafford, to celebrate fifty years of Queen Victoria's reign. The exhibition was open for 166 days and over 4.75 million people passed through the turnstiles. The exhibition demonstrated Manchester's artistic manufacturing skills of the Victorian era. A crystal palace with a 150 ft dome and a nave of 1,020 ft housed the exhibition. The Prince of Wales, later Edward VII, officially opened it.

1933 — In September the Royal Charter for Stretford Borough was presented at Longford Park in Stretford. Sir Albert Smith handed over the Mace to Alderman F W Bates, Deputy Charter Mayor, with Mr Wilfred Trubshaw, Chief Constable (1927-1933), attending.

1941 — On 13 February HM The Queen carried out an inspection of the Special Police at Old Trafford Senior Boys' School.

1954 — On 10 May the new headquarters building in Talbot Road was officially opened amid much public upset at the loss of local stations in Trafford Park, King Street, East Union Street and administration premises in Seymour Grove.

1958 — On 6th February a BEA Elizabethan aircraft carrying Manchester United's team back home from a successful European Cup quarter-final tie crashed whilst attempting to take off from snow-bound Munich Airport. Eight players, three club officials and eight journalists, plus members of the flight crew and friends of the club, lost their lives in the tragedy. The whole of the country, but particularly Manchester, were devastated by the disaster. Tens of

83. One of the early police lock-ups — this one from George Street in Altrincham.

85. *below:* The gravestone of PC Nicholas Cock which is now preserved at the Lancashire Police headquarters at Hutton, along with the bullet that killed him.

84. Superintendent James Bent who served from 1848 until his death in 1901. The photograph is taken from his autobiography "Criminal Life" written in 1890.

thousands of mourners and police officers paid their last respects at Manchester United's ground as the funeral cortege left from the hallowed turf taking the fallen heroes to their final resting place.

1963 — Extra police had to be drafted into the Urmston Show over the August bank holiday weekend to control the crowds of young people who descended for the newly-devised 'Pop Music Festival' being held in the evening. And the main attraction?—The Beatles. On the brink of international stardom, the group had agreed to honour their concert contract — at ten shillings a ticket — which also included Brian Poole and the Tremeloes! Many frenzied girls fainted and became hysterical at the scene. The group were finally hurried out of the show-ground in the same way as they had arrived — in a dust-cart!

1969 — On 26 November over 2,000 police officers paraded for duty around the White City area of Stretford. It was in preparation for the anti-apartheid demonstration which was being held to object to the Rugby Union match between the Springboks from South Africa and the Northern Counties team. Chief Constable Palfreyman of the Lancashire Constabulary had allowed the march to take place providing it was carried out peacefully. Stewards were appointed to police inside the premises and stop people running onto the ground; six cameras were trained on the crowd and police guards were placed at the Wilmslow hotel where the team were staying.

Over 5,000 students from seventeen universities attended the demonstration and there were 172 people arrested and seventy-seven charged with various offences. Two students complained of ill-treatment, there were thirty-six written complaints and twenty letters of congratulations on the manner in which the demonstration had been policed.

1974 — The Local Government reorganisation led to the creation of the Greater Manchester County and with it the Borough of Trafford. The entire area now forms 'M' Division of Greater Manchester Police.

86. Official opening of Altrincham's electric tramways on 9 May 1907.

87. The duty sergeant chatting to a member of the public during Bowdon Wakes week circa 1890s.

Three Guineas Reward.

DROWNED

On Saturday Afternoon, Feb. 26, 1848, about 5 o'clock, in the River Mersey, by the upsetting of a Boat, between Pomona Gardens and Throstle Nest, JOHN THOMAS EYERS, aged 21, dressed in flannel. The above Reward will be paid by Mr. Beswick, Police Office, Town Hall, Manchester, for the Recovery of his Body.

J. Butterworth, Printer, 59, Market-street, Manchester.—378

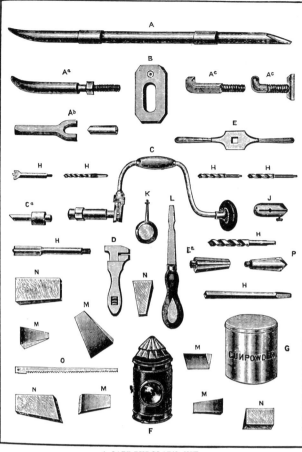

A SAFE-BURGLAR'S KIT.
(*The whole were conveyed in a handbag.*)

A   Little Alderman, or Sectional Jemmy.
Aa Spare Section.
Ab Cleaver end, to be screwed into **A**.
Ac Prisers.
B   Persuasion Plate, for obtaining leverage.
C   American Brace, or Drill.
Ca Centre-bit.
D   Adjustable Spanner.
E   Wrench.
Ea Rimer for Wrench, to enlarge holes.

F   Dark Lantern.
G   Gunpowder.
H   Various Drills, "twist" drills.
J   Lock for Drills (to hold them fast).
K   Oil-can.
L   Screw-driver.
M   Steel Wedges, with razor-like edges.
N   Wooden Wedges.
O   Saw for metal.
P   Countersink.

p. 312.

89. *top left:* A safe-burglar's kit of the 1880s. Charles Peace is known to have carried items similar to some of these shown here.

90. *top right:* Despite outward appearances Charles Peace led a double life — a Sunday School teacher and musician by day but an ingenious and ruthless burglar by night.

91. *bottom left:* Police on Chester Road, Stretford, in readiness for the anti-apartheid demonstration at White City.

92. *bottom right:* 'Beatlemania' comes to Manchester. It was at this time that Manchester gained the reputation of being a 'swinging' city with the many temptations it offered such as coffee bars, clubs, all-night parties and drugs.

BURY
'N' Division

Bury can perhaps be described as the birthplace of policing for it was at Chamber Hall in Bury that Robert Peel, later Sir Robert Peel, Home Secretary, was born on 5 February 1788. The eldest son of wealthy Lancashire textile magnate, Robert Peel senior, the young Peel was educated by James Hargreaves who was the curate of Bury Parish Church. Peel later went on to further education at Harrow and Oxford before entering politics and eventually becoming Home Secretary. He died on 2 July 1850 aged sixty-two but had achieved fame for introducing the Metropolitan Police Act of 1829 which laid the foundations of modern policing as we know it today.

1839 — On 6 November, at a meeting in Preston, magistrates appointed five-hundred constables to form a new Lancashire County Police force. The Chief Constable of the force was to receive £500 per annum while the ordinary constables received eighteen shillings each week. The force was divided into fifteen Divisions. Bury formed one of these Divisions and in charge of each was a superintendent who was paid £100 per annum. At first there were no sergeants and inspectors in the new force but this was soon rectified.

1840 — Despite having an enthusiastic Chief Constable and some early success against crime, the force itself was not popular and magistrates attempted to abolish it, but without success.

The Bury Division superintendent, in line with other Divisions, was allowed to keep a horse to enable him to cover the Division more effectively. An allowance of up to £100 per annum was paid for the upkeep of the horse which was the same salary for the superintendent!

1860s — Originally the constables in Bury wore a blue tail-coat tunic, white trousers and a top-hat as a uniform but in the 1860s changed to wearing a dark blue helmet and closed-neck tunic instead.

1864 — On 9 January PC Luke Charles of the Bury Police was executed for the murder of his wife who had been found drowned in the Pendleton Canal.

1870s — The Chief Constable of Lancashire decided that shaving was bad for the officers' health and encouraged the men to grow beards. By this time working conditions had improved for the police officers but they were still only entitled to one day off a month.

1874 — On 2 February police were called to a large-scale accident at a three-storey building in Paradise Street, Bury, where the third floor had collapsed during a Liberal pre-election meeting. One hundred people fell to the ground of which nine died and sixty were injured.

1876 — Bury became an Incorporated Borough and was thus entitled to form a police force of its own, although this never happened.

94. *right:* Sir Robert Peel, Home Secretary 1822-1827 and 1828-1830, and later Prime Minister.

93. Chamber Hall in Bury where Robert Peel spent his formative years.

'POLICE SOLVE BURY MYSTERY'

1898 — On 1 February Bury Police received information about the death in very suspicious circumstances of a man and woman who were found enveloped in each other's arms at the Derby Hotel in Bury. Police Superintendent Richard Noblett and Sergeant David Keith found little identification at the scene as most of the couple's clothes and papers had been burnt. All that remained was £13 4s 6d (£13.22) to defray funeral expenses, a small amount of clothing which was to be sold to pay the hotel bill, a man's ring engraved *Jacques a LMR 13 mars 1897*, a lady's handkerchief embroidered *MR*, a toothpick marked *Charing Cross Hotel* and a suicide note.

After painstaking police enquires it was found that the trouser buttons had been fitted by a company of London tailors. They said that identification of the client would be on the inside seam of the trousers — subsequently the name John Knight and an address in Rotterdam was found. Apparently Mr Knight was aged forty, was the head of a Rotterdam insurance company, had previously worked for the Turkish and Belgian Consulates, was unmarried, had been born in Holland and had had an English grandfather.

97. *above:* Superintendent Richard Noblett, who led the investigation into the Derby Hotel mystery.

96. Taking the Chief Constable's advice, these officers sport a wide variety of whiskers.

98. The Derby Hotel where the tragedy was discovered.

It was later discovered that the young lady was a Marie Louise Felicie Rousseau who had been born in France in April 1871 and who had been missing from the Rotterdam area for some time. She had been a 'lady of easy virtue' whom Mr Knight had taken into his protection. They had decided that, following family opposition to their wedding plans, they would take their own lives by swallowing prussic acid and their last wish was that they be buried together. Sadly even this was not to be and Mr Knight's body was taken back to Rotterdam whilst his companion was interred in Bury Cemetery.

1915 — On 16 February a new machine at Wrigley's Paper Mill in Bury fell through the floor due to a fault in the roof trusses. Eight people were killed including ex-Police Constable John Sutton from Heap Bridge.

1933 — During the June Whit weekend two major fires occurred. The first one happened at six o'clock on Tuesday, 16 June at Meadowcroft's sweet factory in Pimhole, Bury. Superintendent Blackledge was in charge of the incident and police had to control the large crowds. The premises were burnt to the ground and damage, estimated at £40,000, was said to be "the largest done by fire locally for nearly half a century".

The second fire occurred two hours later at Thomas Mansergh's, a miller and seed merchant business in Haymarket Street, Bury — next to the Corn Market. Fifteen thousand on-lookers watched as the premises were completely gutted, damage being estimated at £30,000 — the second in twelve months.

99. Mansergh's premises before the double fire.

KING'S POLICE MEDALS FOR LOCAL HEROES

1946 — On Friday 20 September three attempts were made to reach ten-year-old Jack Ives of Walmersley Road, Bury, who was stuck half-way along a 375ft flooded culvert 25ft below ground at Pigslee Brow in Bury. The boy had been attempting to jump a 4ft wide culvert when he slipped and fell and was swept into the 6ft wide culvert pipe, the water pressure of which was running through at a rate of 123,000 gallons a minute. He managed to get a foothold halfway along the culvert just above a 5ft waterfall.

PC's Ray Wilde, Henry Simmonds and Arnold Rotherham attended the scene and a Mr Thomas Lee of Beswick in Manchester assisted.

PC Wilde and Mr Lee found a manhole at the junction of another culvert which was bringing in a further 62,000 gallons of water a minute into the mains pipe. Roped together they descended the 25ft to the culvert level and Mr Lee attached himself firmly to the bottom of the iron rungs and paid out the line while PC Windle struggled to keep a foothold in the rushing water. Three times attempts were made but finally abandoned.

A message was sent to Divisional headquarters in Tenterden Street for more rope and an empty oil drum which was attached to one end of the new rope and floated down the culvert. In the meantime young Jack was shouting to let them know he was still safe.

When the drum reached the lower end of the culvert the rope was secured at both ends and, using it to drag themselves along, PC's Simmonds and Rotherham made their way along the pipe. They passed the waterfall by climbing iron stanchions set into concrete and PC Simmonds clung to these with a torch in his hand so that PC Rotherham had enough light to locate the boy. All three then made their way to safety and were rushed to Bury Infirmary suffering from shock.

The three officers later received King's Police Medals (PC Simmonds' second).

1952 — On 23 January a railway footbridge collapsed at Knowsley Street in Bury. It involved Blackburn Rovers supporters who were waiting for the train which would take them home after a Gigg Lane match. When the footbridge collapsed many fell onto the track and two-hundred people were injured. A bigger disaster was averted when the oncoming train only two-hundred yards away was stopped from ploughing into the horrific scene.

After the disaster the Minister of Transport held a public enquiry into the safety regulations governing such bridges.

1968 — Early on Sunday morning, 17 November, a major fire occurred in Bury when the sixty-seven year old market building was completely destroyed within nine minutes. Police set up a control point plus road diversions and it is reported that the fire could be seen for many miles.

1974 — With Local Government reorganisation Bury became 'N' Division of Greater Manchester Police.

100. Bury's historic market hall — destroyed by fire in only nine minutes.

101. Members of Bury Division of Lancashire Constabulary marching past Sir Robert Peel's statue in 1961.

ROCHDALE
'P' Division

Although counties were allowed to set up their own police forces from 1839 onwards, it was not until 11 March 1857 that Rochdale Borough Police was formed. Their first Chief Officer was Mr John Henry Callender and he commanded a force of fifteen officers with six of his officers acting as lamp-lighters.

The style of dress of the new force was a blue swallow-tail frock-coat with bright buttons, blue trousers, a tall hat with a leather top, a leather collar-stock and a brass-buckled belt. In cold weather a great-coat and a cloth cape were issued. Every man was given a 6d (2.5p) boot allowance and a printed set of instructions.

1859 — The Watch Committee established a Superannuation Fund so as to provide a pension for the officers.

1863 — Chief Officer Callender resigned to be followed by Lieutenant William Sylvester, aged only twenty. One of the notable cases he had to deal with was the stealing of bodies from graveyards.

1866 — Mr Sylvester moved on to Salford, being replaced by Captain Roland Davies, a controversial appointee who had no previous police experience. A noteworthy aspect of Mr Davies' tenure was the Murphy rioting of 1866-1868 against the priesthood which occurred in the Rochdale area and around the country.

1869 — Mr Samuel Stevens of Chesterfield succeeded Mr Davies at a salary of £175 per year.

1870s — Detectives were given a three shillings allowance in lieu of clothing.

During the early part of this decade, an area of central Rochdale was a den of vice, prostitution and crime but a concerted police effort soon cleared this up.

1872 — Police headquarters were transferred from Union Street to the town hall.

1877 — The fire brigade was attached to the police service and several policemen were trained and equipped to serve as firemen.

1878 — Three Canal Constables were appointed.

1881 — Mr Stevens left the force and was replaced by Mr Joseph Wilkinson, from Kendal, at a salary of £250.

1882 — The first telephone was installed at the station. In the same year Mr Wilkinson set up a police band which was very popular in the town until it was wound-up in 1918.

During the 1880s the Police Fire Brigade occasionally attended fires outside the borough boundary thereby leaving Rochdale deprived of police protection. In 1891 the HM Inspectorate threatened to withhold the Certificate of Efficiency unless the practise ceased.

1893 — Mr Wilkinson was replaced by Mr Charles Buck. During this time Rochdale was troubled by 'garrotte robberies', a peculiar form of street crime in which victims were strangled.

1898 — Mr Leonard Campbell Barry was appointed as Chief Constable. A progressive man, he established at Rochdale a central clearing-house for criminal records. He also introduced police dogs.

1908 — Rochdale Police Fire Brigade became the first in the country to own a motorised fire engine.

1917 — Mr Barry resigned due to ill-health and was replaced by Mr Henry Howarth from Liverpool.

1920s — During this period Rochdale Police started a 'Down and Out' fund for vagrants.

102. *top right:* John Henry Callender, first Chief Officer of Rochdale Borough Police force, 1857-1863.

103. Fear of 'Resurrectionists' led to the enclosing of some graves with protective iron railings, many of which can still be seen today.

1926 — Rochdale purchased its first motor vehicle — an AJS motor-cycle combination.

1927 — Rochdale Police were pioneers of wireless telegraphy and purchased their first apparatus during the year.

1929 — Twenty-two call boxes were introduced for use by both police and public.

1930s — As a response to the threat of war, an Air Raid Precaution Department was formed including two hundred Special Constables.

1939 — On 1 April another sports ground disaster occurred, this time during the Salford v Leigh Rugby League Cup semi-final at Rochdale Hornet's athletic ground. On this occasion two people died and seventeen were injured of the 40,000-strong crowd. Sir Samuel Hoare, Home Secretary, said: "The roof collapsed under the weight of persons who had persisted in climbing onto it, in spite of the efforts of the police to prevent it."

1941 — In March two policemen, Detective Inspector Henry Stables and Detective Sergeant Thomas Dale, were killed in a cellar below a shop. A youth had stolen some explosives and firearms from a military depot and set up a booby-trap.

1945 — Mr Howarth retired after forty-one years' service, to be replaced by Major Sidney Joseph Harvey who had just left the Armed forces.

1946 — Rochdale's first female officers were appointed.

1957 — The force had increased to 178 officers.

1958 — Mr Frank Stanley Gale was appointed Chief Constable.

1964 — Mr Patrick Ross was appointed Chief Constable.

1969 — Rochdale Constabulary became part of Lancashire Constabulary.

1974 — On amalgamation into Greater Manchester Police Rochdale became part of the 'P' Division.

104. Detective officers from the Rochdale Borough Police in 1875.

105. The Rochdale Motorcycle Section around 1930 with their versatile three-man side-car combinations.

106. Mayhem following the Hornets' stand collapse in April 1939.

107. *left:* Detective Inspector Stables as a young PC.

108. A relief going on duty in Rochdale in the 1950s. The officer third from the left is PC Fred Llewellyn (retired GMP 1978) and the one on the extreme right is PC Alan Collison (retired GMP 1980).

OLDHAM
'Q' Division

Before 1826 Justices of the Peace, appointed by the Crown from amongst the more notable members of Oldham, engaged parish constables to look after law and order. These constables also performed other duties. For example in 1616 the constables received and dispensed of all public monies including the poor relief. In 1718 they were responsible for the military training of the parishioners and they had charge of the parish armour which was kept at the church.

Fear of civil unrest in 1819 caused the Oldham Yeoman Cavalry to be placed on duty for a month. Special Constables were sworn-in to perform night duty which was called 'Watch and Ward'.

On 26 May 1826 Royal Assent was given to "an act for paving, watching, lighting, cleansing and improving the township of Oldham in the County of Lancaster and for regulating the police thereof". This brought into being police Commissioners from 1 January 1827. The police Commissioners were not elected but were appointed. They had to be male and pay £30 in rent or receive £50 a year from property. For a number of years after 1827 the responsibility for street lighting devolved upon the police. The lamp-lighters were not only to light lamps but were required to train as firemen and had to be willing to act as policemen at busy times and on a Sunday.

109. *right:* A poster to advertise the Coronation of Queen Victoria in 1838. Leading Oldham's celebratory procession were the beadles and deputy constable of the township.
110. The Inspector of the Weights and Measures Department together with the tools of his trade.

In 1841 the Commissioners built the town hall at a cost of £4,810; this was for what is now the front section of the building which was later extended. Police arrangements there were unsatisfactory and they caused much controversy. Policing was not adequately carried out and in 1848 the magistrates decided to invite the County force to police Oldham. This was greatly resented by many people; the Justices were bringing in outsiders to police them, whereas the Commissioners had been appointing local constables. Captain John Woodford, the Chief Constable of Lancashire, brought in the County Police on 29 June 1849 and installed his men in the town hall as was his official right. However, the Commissioners told him he could only occupy four cells and an office.

1849 — On 13 June a Charter of Incorporation was received and Oldham became a borough. One of the first duties of the newly-elected town council was to form a police force. On 26 October the Council resolved to appoint a Watch Committee and organised a police force. Notification was sent to Captain Woodford that his men were no longer required.

The new force consisted of a superintendent, John Jackson, a sergeant and ten constables. There was no post of Chief Constable. The twelve men were to look after a population of 50,000. The salary of the superintendent was £100 a year, the sergeant received £78 and the constables earned £52 a year. The sergeant was to be married and live rent-free at the town hall but his pay also secured the services of his wife. No constable was to be more than thirty-six years old and he had to be 5ft 8ins or over. He had to be able to read, write and keep accounts. It also required that the constable be free from all bodily complaints, of a strong constitution, civil and generally intelligent. He should abstain from any expressions, political or religious, calculated to give offence and obey all orders from his superiors and on no account be allowed to vote in elections on pain of dismissal.

Several of the Chief Constables of Oldham went on to larger forces. One of the most famous was Robert Peacock who became one of Manchester's most outstanding Chief Constables.

With the help of Special Constables whenever they were needed, especially during the two World Wars, the small force managed to keep law and order in the borough.

1921 — The first policewoman, Clara Walkden, was appointed. At that time, only Lancashire had sworn-in women constables.

1949 — In its centenary year Oldham Borough had a force of 203, including six policewomen.

1959 — A communications room was opened at the police headquarters in the town hall.

1967 — Negotiations began on the amalgamation of the borough force into the County Constabulary. One of the last acts of the old borough police was to move into its new headquarters building, opposite the modern council office block in the centre of the town.

1969 — On 1 April Oldham, along with twelve other forces, became part of Lancashire County.

1974 — The former borough force became 'Q' Division of the newly-created Greater Manchester Police.

111. The old Royton police station.

112. A break in post-war austerity was provided by Oldham Police centenary celebrations in 1949.

113. The Roll of Honour commemorating the Oldham police officers who served in the First World War, transferred from its original site in the town hall building to the foyer of the present-day Oldham headquarters.

GMP Today

Greater Manchester Police came into existence on 1 April 1974 upon amalgamation with areas of Manchester and Salford, Lancashire, Cheshire and West Yorkshire, making it the largest provincial force in England and Wales. At that time it had an establishment of 6,628 officers with an actual strength of 5,545 officers and 1,796 civilian staff, and dealt with 102,144 crimes reported to the police.

The amalgamation followed Local Government reorganisation throughout the country. A Force Advisory Group was set up in June 1972 comprising senior police officers from those areas in and around Manchester affected by the changes. The new areas to be policed covered a total of almost 500 square miles with a population of 2.75 million inhabitants.

From the outset it was agreed that administrative, personnel and other services, including traffic and CID, would be centrally-controlled by five Assistant Chief Constables from force headquarters in Manchester City's Southmill Street. The City of Manchester was to be divided into five separate police areas to be known as A-E Divisions with their Divisional headquarters in A-City, B-Collyhurst, C-Bradford, D-Longsight and E-Rusholme. The boundaries of the nine outer territorial Divisions would be co-terminus with those of the local Metropolitan Borough Councils, thus F-Salford, G-Tameside, J-Stockport, K-Bolton, L-Wigan, M-Trafford, N-Bury, P-Rochdale and Q-Oldham. Two years later the 'D' Division of the force took over the policing of Manchester International Airport.

Upon amalgamation on 1 April 1974 the Greater Manchester Police Authority, comprising councillors and magistrates representing the Greater Manchester area, replaced the old Watch Committee.

The first Chief Constable of GMP was Mr William James Richards, the former Deputy Chief Constable of the Manchester and Salford force. He took over the force at a time when there was unprecedented growth in crime such as murder, manslaughter, robbery and assault. Newer crimes such as large-scale drug trafficking, hi-jacking of expensively-laden lorries and armed raids on stores and building societies also threatened the fabric of local life. It was finally decided to set up specialised police squads to attempt to tackle these problems, often liaising at a national level, and the success of these squads in combatting many forms of high-level crime continues today. Within five days of amalgamation, the new force was put to the test when on 6 April the IRA planted bombs at the Manchester Magistrates' Courts, resulting in many deaths and injuries.

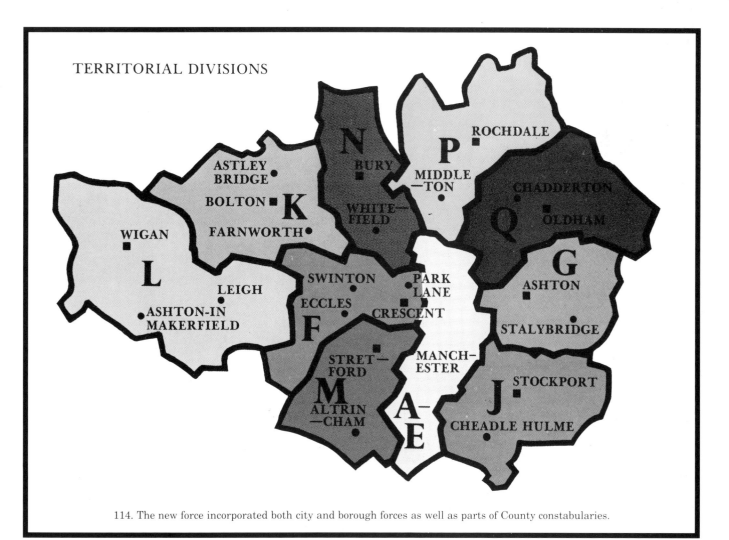

TERRITORIAL DIVISIONS

114. The new force incorporated both city and borough forces as well as parts of County constabularies.

115a. The devastation after the 1974 IRA bombing at the Manchester Magistrates' Courts.

115b. On 27 January 1975, in a three-week spate of IRA bombings in Manchester, an incendiary device was planted in the basement of Lewis's store, injuring nineteen people and causing thousands of pounds worth of damage.

On 1 July 1976 Mr Cyril James Anderton became the new Chief Constable of GMP, having served as the Deputy Chief Constable for eight months. From the outset Mr Anderton adopted a policy of 'public accountability' and steered the force towards closer contact with the public, introducing many new initiatives to promote his beliefs. One such step was the establishment of the Community Contact Departments to foster good relationships with the public through school talks and many other community relations events.

During this and the ensuing years, there were major changes in the force. In 1976 the Hough End site in Chorlton-cum-Hardy was opened as the main kennels and stables for GMP's dogs and horses, as well as becoming the home of the central Sports and Social Club for the force.

On 8 October 1977 Greater Manchester Police had to control a National Front march in Hyde. Over 6,000 officers from several forces were involved and the whole operation cost around £140,000.

Due to the size of GMP and the demands for quicker and better efficiency it was decided that a new headquarters would have to be provided to house, under one roof, the main administrative functions of the force — rather than have them fragmented over many buildings. Chester House in Stretford, a speculative office block, had therefore been purchased in 1976, and took over two years to prepare before staff moved in during January 1979. The building was officially opened by HRH The Princess Anne on 30 May that year.

In 1980 GMP took over the Sedgley Park Teacher Training College in Prestwich as its new residential force training school, moving from its previous building at Peterloo House in the city centre, which was on the site of the Peterloo Massacre of 1819.

Similarly land at Openshaw, which had been purchased in 1973, was transformed into the force's central stores, workshops and Traffic Services Branch, with the three phases being completed by 1981.

On 22 February 1980 thirty-two officers from GMP were flown to Rhodesia to assist in supervising the General Elections which marked the end of the Rhodesian Government's Unilateral Declaration of Independence.

The summer of 1981 was over-shadowed by outbreaks of serious public disorder in areas around the country. In particular between 8-12 July there was rioting and criminal damage throughout Greater Manchester but primarily centering around the Moss Side area. This led to 241 people being arrested in Moss Side and a further 229 arrested elsewhere in the force area.

The year 1982 was memorable for many reasons, not least of which was the visit of His Holiness Pope John Paul II to Heaton Park in Manchester. Careful planning of the whole event by GMP ensured that the visit was a resounding success, especially in view of it being the largest public event ever policed in the area.

However, 1982 was also the year when two GMP officers — DC John Sandford based at Manchester Airport and PC John Egerton from Farnworth — were fatally injured on duty.

On 25 September that year a huge explosion occurred in premises storing chemicals in Flax Street, Salford. One hundred and fifty officers attended and carried out a general evacuation, ten of whom were hospitalised as a result of breathing poisonous fumes.

On 1 May 1983 GMP introduced the Lay Visitors' Scheme throughout the force area. This allowed members of

116. On 1 July 1976 Mr Anderton, at 42 years of age, became the youngest-ever Chief Constable (at that time) and is the tenth in the Manchester force's history.

117. On 20 January 1977 fire broke out at factory premises in China Lane in central Manchester, killing seven women workers.

118. Few Manchester people could ever forget the tragic fire of May 1979 which started in the furniture department of Woolworth's and killed ten people.

119. *right:* The Hough End complex which was opened in 1976.

120. Police officers escorting Martin Webster of the National Front in October 1977.

121-122. *left:* The completed Chester House before staff moved in during January 1979. *above:* HRH Princess Anne officially opened GMP's prestigious new headquarters in May that year.

123. *below:* The GMP contingent of officers on their way to Rhodesia.

125. The new Openshaw complex opened in 1981.

126. Police in riot protection gear during the Moss Side riots

127. A special moment in the life of Policewoman Suzanne Gagie as she meets His Holiness Pope John Paul II

128. *above:* The Flax Street premises after the blaze which caused over £1.6 million damage.

129. *bottom left:* The memorial tablets to GMP officers who have died on duty provides a poignant sight in the HQ reception area.

130. *bottom right:* The Police and Criminal Evidence Act — a major landmark in police history.

Police and Criminal Evidence Act 1984

CHAPTER 60

131. Holding back pickets at Salford's Agecroft Colliery in 1984.

132. The year 1984 saw a rail disaster in the Weaste area of Salford when the Liverpool to Scarborough express passenger train crashed into the rear of a slow-moving tanker. The adjacent M602 motorway had to be closed and residents in nearby houses were evacuated due to the danger of explosion. The train driver and a passenger were killed and 81 of the 200 passengers required hospital treatment.

the County Council to visit people detained in police custody to ensure their rights were being observed. Similarly, the Police and Criminal Evidence Act 1984 which took effect in 1986 had wide-ranging effects on police powers. It also meant a major refurbishment programme to standardise stations in accordance with PACE regulations.

The national Miners' Strike was a dominant feature of 1984 and put great strain on GMP's resources. The police aspect of the strike was under the direction of the National Reporting Centre at Scotland Yard and members of GMP were dispatched to various parts of the country to assist other forces. Despite having several pits to police in their own area, GMP did not require assistance from members of any other forces at any point during the dispute.

On 22 August 1985 a major tragedy occurred at Manchester Airport when a British Airtours Boeing 737 aeroplane burst into flames on take-off, killing fifty-five people. Officers and civilian staff from GMP dealt magnificently with the ensuing carnage which attracted world-wide attention.

Her Majesty the Queen graced the force on 21 March 1986 when she officially opened the new Communications and Computer Centre at Chester House Phase II. This purpose-built complex alongside the Chester House headquarters building is one of the most advanced units of its kind in Great Britain and will ensure efficient communications and information processing by the force into the twenty-first century.

The year 1986 also saw the abolition of the Metropolitan County tier of Local Government and Greater Manchester Council was wound-up on 31 March. The administrative functions of the former Council were shared between the local borough councils and there were many changes in the membership of the Police Authority.

In 1987 there was the horrific discovery on the bleak Saddleworth Moors of the body of sixteen-year-old Pauline Reed from Gorton who had disappeared from home in July 1963. The body had been one of the infamous Moors Murders committed by Myra Hindley and Ian Brady and involved searching and digging in the area for many months.

One of the most unforgettable incidents in Manchester's aviation history occurred on Tuesday evening, 7 June 1988, when a Max Holste super-light aircraft crash-landed on the eastbound carriageway of the M62 motorway at Eccles. Three vehicles were hit, one of which had its roof sliced off, but mercifully only one person received serious injuries in the accident.

Today, GMP has over 7,000 officers and 2,259 civilian staff spread over its fourteen territorial Divisions and six administrative Departments throughout the force. It manages 102 police buildings and has over 1,000 vehicles in its fleet.

However, despite all the massive changes which have taken place in the 150 years since Manchester received its Incorporation, the main objective now, as then, is to preserve and protect its people and keep the Queen's peace at all times.

133. Officers sifting through the wreckage of the Manchester air disaster in which 55 people lost their lives.

134. HM the Queen officially unveiling the commemorative plaque in the Chester House Phase II building.

135. Chief Superintendent Peter Topping leading the gruesome hunt for the bodies of the two missing children on Saddleworth Moor above Oldham.

136. Police and fire officers at the scene of the M62 motorway air crash in June 1988.

The Way We Were

UNIFORMS, HELMETS AND EQUIPMENT

Uniforms

It is only in comparatively recent times that officers of the law have worn a recognisable uniform.

In medieval times the local constable of a village had merely his staff of office to indicate his position in the community.

By the eighteenth century some attempt at uniform was made in the larger towns. In Manchester the beadle wore a yellow jersey coat and hat and carried a staff with a gilded top. Lock-up keepers in the town wore a brown coat edged in red. The Bow Street horse patrol in London, first used by Sir John Fielding, wore a blue coat with yellow buttons, blue trousers, black boots, tall leather hat, white gloves and scarlet waistcoat — which gave them the nickname of 'Robin Redbreasts'. The tradition of blue coats was followed by Peel's new Metropolitan Police force of 1829. The 'Peelers' wore a blue tail coat with blue trousers for winter and white trousers for summer. On their heads they wore a reinforced top-hat. Generally they wore a belt and in this they carried the rick or wooden rattle that was used to call for help. A truncheon was normally carried in a pocket in the tail of the coat. This style of uniform was later adopted in most parts of the country, although officers in Salford initially wore green uniforms while those in Wigan preferred brown.

These early constables were required to wear uniform during all waking hours, on or off duty, and so to indicate whether the officer was on duty or not, a striped band, the duty band, was worn on the lower left sleeve and removed when going off duty.

In Manchester a Peeler-style uniform of a closed frock-coat and top-hat was worn up to the 1860s, while in the Lancashire County area top-hat and tails were replaced in the 1850s with a peaked-cap with a high flared crown. A new style was on its way from London, however, and it marked a change in the police image.

In 1864 the Metropolitan Police issued a new helmet and tunic uniform. The helmet, virtually the same as the 'County' style of today, was based partly on the militia pattern helmets, while the tunic was closely styled on the Grenadiers' tunic cut long and with eight buttons and no pockets. A belt was worn with the tunic and on this was hung the officer's 'Bulls-Eye Lantern' at night. A whistle was also issued for the first time. The truncheon was no longer concealed but carried in a leather tube suspended from the belt. Onto this belt, in times of disorder in the 1860s, went cutlasses and occasionally pistol holsters and ammunition.

The new uniform was inspired by military fashion and set a trend in police clothing which was to last well into this century. Dark blue was retained as the standard colour, perhaps because dirt was more easily concealed; certainly the smoky oil-lamps carried on the belt could leave soot stains on tunic and officer.

137. *top:* A Salford Peeler about 1850.

138. A police constable equipped for night duty in 1889.

139. *above:* PC Ken Taylor and PC George Blackwood use their capes to shelter a small spectator when the King visited Manchester in May 1938.

140. *right:* The braided tunic and pill-box hat worn by an Oldham inspector prior to the First World War.

141. The uniforms worn by these London policewomen post-1918 were copied by the early provincial Policewomen's Departments.

In wet or cold weather a cape was generally worn, sometimes over a greatcoat. As nearly all officers patrolled on foot, the insulation provided by the heavy woollen melton cloth was most welcome. On very cold nights it was not unknown for the lamps to be worn under the cape, although it generally meant parading-off with a soot-covered face.

By the twentieth century most forces had adopted the helmet and tunic of the Metropolitan Police, although in the cities and boroughs a combed helmet, similar to the one worn in Greater Manchester today, could be found. By the First World War most forces issued a modified tunic with five or six buttons and two breast pockets. The tunic was worn without a belt and so the older tunic with belt was retained for night duty, with black buttons and black facings for the helmet.

Senior officers above the rank of sergeant generally wore a braided tunic or frock-coat until the late 1920s. Initially a pill-box hat was worn with the uniform, later being replaced by a peaked cap.

The first female police officers wore a long skirt with an open-necked tunic and a white blouse and black tie. After the Second World War, while skirts shortened, tunics remained much the same. In the 1960s a new uniform designed by Norman Hartnell was widely worn and set the style in women's uniforms for many years. The trouser suit was introduced from the mid-1970s primarily for wear during night duty and winter months.

Currently Greater Manchester Police male officers wear a dark blue beltless tunic with pockets and an open neck, matching trousers, black tie and a pale blue or white shirt depending upon their rank, while women officers wear a dark open-necked pocketless tunic and either a matching skirt or trousers, a white shirt and black and white chequered bow-style cravat.

142. Policewomen parading down Manchester's Deansgate in the early 1970s wearing the 'Hostess-style' hat with the detachable waterproof white cover, which was removed for night duty.

143. *bottom left:* PW Sandra McGuirk of the Traffic Department, modelling the new trouser suit.

144. *below:* Epaulette insignia worn by regular officers in GMP.

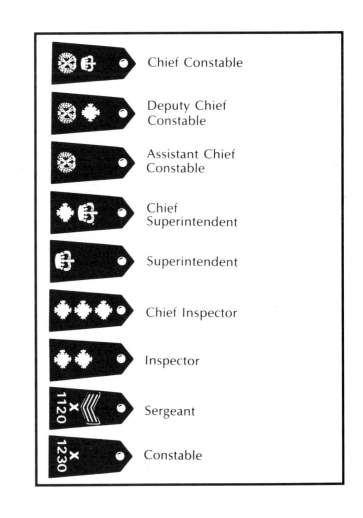

Chief Constable

Deputy Chief Constable

Assistant Chief Constable

Chief Superintendent

Superintendent

Chief Inspector

Inspector

Sergeant

Constable

145a-b. Police officers wearing the uniform of 1989.

146. A cross-section of helmet styles. back row, left to right: Salford City Police helmet of the 1960s and Cheshire 'Shako' hat of the 1920s. front row: Manchester City Police helmets of the 1920s, comprising combed style, summer issue and Mounted Section ceremonial.

Helmets

Police helmets first came on the scene in London in the mid-1860s and, together with the new shorter tunic, replaced the former top-hat and frock-coat common in most forces since 1829.

Not all forces were quick to adopt the new headgear for, while Lancashire sported the new helmets, Manchester officers had to put up with the old topper. A poem of the time survives and makes it clear that Manchester men were not happy. Called *The Manchester Police Hat* one verse runs:

I would a County constable I were and not a city
policeman,
I would burn it and a helmet mount instead;
No more a mournful object then for universal pity;
I would have what should protect, as well as decorate
my head.
So down with the hat! the old policeman scarecrow
And give instead a helmet that will let the wearer's
hair grow
And shield his head from damage in the fury of the
fray.
(Nov 1869).

The new helmets were styled on various military patterns. The style known as the comb helmet worn in GMP today appears to have been based on Cavalry helmets while the 'bobble' style worn up to 1968 in Salford was inspired by the 'Home pattern' helmet of the Army. So striking was the resemblance to a military uniform that on one occasion a militia man, returning home in full blue uniform and helmet, noted that children hid from him and people sought his help assuming he was a police officer.

In the early days many different styles of helmet were produced, some more practical than others. In Manchester woven straw helmets with a dark blue cloth cover were issued in summer while in other areas they were left uncovered in natural straw. Some helmets were festooned with chain link chin-straps and elaborate ventilator pieces including spikes, globes and rosettes.

In parts of Cheshire, such as Altrincham and Stockport, officers continued to wear the 'Shako'-style of stiffened cloth cap until the late 1920s instead of a standard helmet. Another striking style of helmet was that worn by Salford Police until 1968. This was a cloth-covered helmet with a metal globe on top, also available in white for point duty, and is today a much sought-after collectors' item.

Protection does not always seem to have been the priority and local taste and display remained a key to helmet design well into the 1960s. Increasingly as the twentieth century wore on helmets were being made of the now familiar strengthened felt construction but, although they were stronger than straw or cork, they could still become floppy after prolonged soaking in the rain. Incidently, a Manchester order to constables in 1908 stresses that chin straps should be worn down at all times, otherwise "the helmet could not perform the function for which it was intended".

In Manchester there were two styles of helmet worn concurrently in the early twentieth century. The first was the straw helmet worn in summer and a combed helmet made of felt and almost identical to the modern version. There was also a third variation which was the night helmet, once again a combed version but with all the facings and the helmet plate painted black. A night helmet was still being issued in many forces up to the early 1970s.

148. For traffic point duty Salford provided a full white uniform with matching helmet.

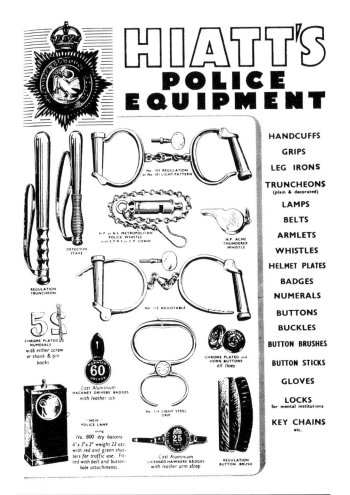

149. The earlier ventilation piece (left) compared with the post-1938 version.

As far as facings are concerned, only two styles of ventilator have been used on Manchester comb helmets. The earlier one was decorated with birds' wings and had three circular holes for ventilation, while the modern version has bats' (or dragons?) wings and three triangular holes. The changeover took place about 1938 when the new star-shaped helmet plate was introduced.

Traditionally white metal has been used for helmet facings but in addition brass, silver-plated brass and enamel have all been used. Merseyside Police have since gone one stage further by issuing plastic helmet plates to prevent a metal plate being driven through the helmet into the skull, a problem highlighted as early as the 1870s soon after their introduction.

A wide-brimmed hat was worn by the early policewomen but after the Second World War this was replaced by a soft cap.

In the 1960s the new uniform designed by Norman Hartnell included a pill-box hat but by the mid-1980s a bowler-style 'Pathfinder' helmet was introduced for policewomen to give greater protection than the earlier soft caps.

Today's male officers of constable and sergeant rank wear a dark-blue combed helmet with enamelled helmet plate, whereas senior male officers wear a flat cap with a badge. Various braidings on the hat to denote rank are used for both male and female officers.

Truncheons

The term 'truncheon' is derived from the old French word 'trunchon' meaning a short club or cudgel, and has been carried by watchmen, parish constables and latterly police officers since the Middle Ages. Gradually the truncheon became recognised as not merely a means of defence but also a symbol of authority.

Eighteenth century truncheons frequently carried a borough coat of arms or the cypher of the reigning Monarch. They would often be produced at the time of an arrest as proof of identity as the early parish constables often wore no special uniform and the truncheon was usually their sole symbol of office.

With the coming of the modern police in 1829, a truncheon some 20 ins long was issued and carried in the tail of the officer's uniform coat. In 1856 truncheons were shortened to about 17ins and were generally carried in a leather case fixed to the belt. Further changes in the uniform gave rise to the close-neck tunic which was the same length as a modern jacket.

In 1887 the Commissioner of the Metropolitan Police gave orders that truncheons were to be carried in a modified trouser pocket so as to make them less conspicuous. Other forces followed suit and this is still the universal practise today.

Specialised truncheons were also produced, the most common being a longer version of between 21ins and 36ins issued to mounted police. A shortened version of some 12ins in length was available for detective officers. Policewomen are not generally issued with truncheons although some carry a version of the detective's truncheon in a shoulder bag.

Woods such as rosewood, oak, lignum-vitae and ash have all been used for making truncheons and normally a leather strap is attached at the grip-end to afford a more secure hold.

In the Victorian times some experimental truncheons were produced for there was at the time no agreement as to what was the best defensive weapon to issue to police. Some were very large and heavy and a small number were even made of cast iron. One of these iron truncheons contained a knife blade which slid out of the top of the truncheon. The base of the weapon was hollow and could be screwed onto a pole for defence against hostile crowds. Another inventor designed a truncheon with a pistol barrel attached! It is most unlikely that any of these outrageous devices were ever issued to police officers.

The use of the truncheon has always been strictly controlled as this extract from a 1908 police manual makes clear: "It must not be resorted to except in extreme cases when all other attempts have failed and a prisoner is likely to escape through the constable having been ill-used or overpowered".

Many officers refer to their truncheon as a 'staff', but strictly speaking the staff is the walking-stick carried by sergeants and inspectors. Returning to the 'Staff of Office' of the ancient parish constables, the sergeant's version is generally in plain turned wood while the inspector's traditionally had a silver top. Tapped on paving stones, the noise of the staff could be heard a mile away and would announce the sergeant's presence or summon assistance. Some staffs are carried today but purely as a symbol of office.

150. Three Victorian truncheons which often had the name of the force or the officer's collar number printed on them. The truncheon on the left is the ceremonial one which was carried by the head constable of Ardwick prior to 1838.

Tipstaves

Developing side-by-side with the truncheon was the tipstaff which dates from the late Middle Ages.

The tipstaff was never used for defence and takes the form of a hollow tube, generally about 6ins long. In the early days it was sometimes made in wood or ivory and later examples were usually in brass or silver. On top of the tipstaff was the crown of the reigning Monarch and gradually they became recognised as symbols of authority. The tipstaff could be unscrewed and a warrant could be served simply by tapping the person on the shoulder.

The Bow Street Runners normally carried their name and number on a document carried in a tipstaff and later Metropolitan constables continued this practise until the first warrant cards were issued in the 1870s. However, senior London detectives continued to carry tipstaves until they were withdrawn in 1887.

151. A brass tipstaff dated 1841 unscrewed into its two sections.

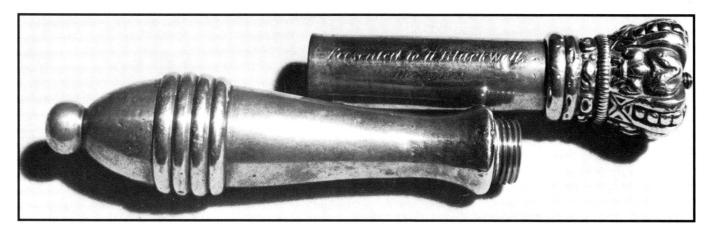

152. The early style of Manchester warrant card for Inspector Palmer who was appointed in 1856. By the 1960s these cards were issued with a photograph of the officer, rank and signature.

Handcuffs and Snaps

Handcuffs were in use long before the formation of the first police forces and were normally used to restrain violent prisoners.

Most handcuffs locked automatically when closed around the wrist of the prisoner and had to be released by means of a screw-in key. Each cuff was marked with the number of the key that opened it.

Modern handcuffs are extremely strong and only half the weight of the old screw-type versions.

'Snaps' which were used by Manchester Police had no key and were released by lifting the metal tab on the closed side. Only one wrist of the prisoner could be restrained and the policeman had to keep hold of the other end.

Bell, Rattle, Lantern and Lamps

Communication and illumination have always played an important role in policing, the hue and cry being the earliest method of raising the alarm and flame torches lighting the way.

The carrying of a bell, lantern and a rattle symbolised the work of the early night watchmen or 'Charlies' and in fact in 1653 Manchester itself insisted that its own watchmen provide a bell to ring every hour.

Gradually other portable methods were introduced such as the modernised 'Bulls Eye Lantern' and candle, battery and accumulator lamps.

In 1912 the electric lamp was introduced and by 1921 the Metropolitan Police were issued with Optalyte electric lanterns. By 1923 the 'Wootton' lamp emerged as a greatly-improved waterproof lantern which could give out twelve hours of continuous light. Around the same time small pocket torches started to be issued to inspectors.

The whistle was introduced in the late 1860s and can still be worn on the modern police tunic if desired. However, its effectiveness has been over-taken by the wearing of personal radios which give a much better and quicker response to calls for assistance.

153. Three types of handcuffs. *top*:Pair of Manchester 'snaps'. *left*: Screw key-style handcuffs. *right*: Adjustable modern ratchet-type handcuffs. They are all surrounded by a set of prison van leg irons.
154. *below:* The evolution of police lamps. *back row, left to right:* The Bull's Eye lantern and candle lamp from 1890. *front row:* 1960s battery lamp, a modern rubber torch and 1920s 'Wootton' battery light.

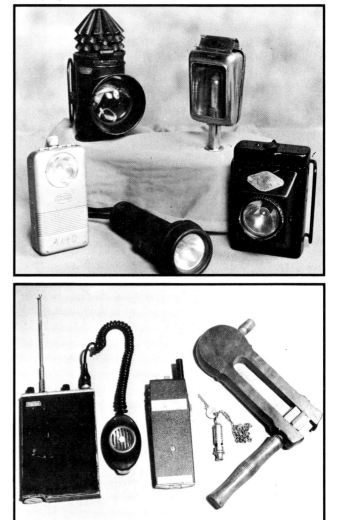

155. *right:* Keeping in touch. left to right: The heavy personal radio set of the 1950s/early 1960s which was later replaced by the slimmer version used today. centre: The whistle and chain here has a key used for access to the police/public telephone box. right: The rattle carried by both night watchmen and early Peelers.

COMMUNICATIONS

In 1663 the City of London began to employ night watchmen who were equipped with a bell, lantern and rattle. From a decade earlier Manchester's own watchmen had started to carry a bell to ring every hour and would state the time and weather.

When the new police forces were introduced they adopted the wooden rattle as a means of raising the alarm. From 1829 until the 1920s the paraffin-powered 'Bulls Eye Lantern', a silent form of communication, was used as well as the gradual introduction of candle, battery and accumulator lamps. During the late 1860s the whistle took over from the rattle although its usage became less popular once personal radios became commonplace.

The telegraph system was developed in the 1830s and by 1870 all important stations were connected to Scotland Yard. The first telephone was installed in Scotland Yard in 1883. By 1898 the police telephone system was put on the public telephone exchange.

In 1923 the police box system was introduced in Sunderland and by 1928 Manchester had one of its own. This system involved the construction of numerous police boxes which were relatively cheap to build and run and were to replace many of the old stations. Each box had telephones for public and police use and were to serve as a mini-station. However they were not popular with policemen and never replaced the stations. They were kept as an addition to the police system and an important part of the communications network up until the 1960s.

Police pillars, cast-iron structures with a telephone box and light on top, were introduced in 1936 and played a similar role to the police boxes as far as communications were concerned. These also had two telephones.

157. It was through switchboards like this that the public could first speak to the police by telephone.

158. PC Harry Knowles makes a call from Manchester's first police box at Ben Brierley on Moston Lane, Moston.

156. The rattle carried by this watchman can be seen tucked into the cross-belt, which is also used to carry a cutlass.

159. In the transition period between replacing many old and decaying police stations and building new ones, stringent economy measures led to a bold experiment in 'new technology'. Officers in many areas used the police box system for booking on and off by telephone to their Divisional headquarters. However, drinking water and toilet facilities were a distinct problem and it was not uncommon to see an officer carrying his 'billy can' in search of 'Corporation pop'. Fortunately this Manchester box seems to have found the perfect answer . . . !

The police had its first wireless installations in 1922 and a year later wireless was used to successfully control traffic at Epsom Derby. Mobile transmitter experiments, where a wireless was put in a van, date from this time.

By 1929 the Metropolitan Flying Squad had fast cars, each with a detachable wireless. Morse code was used as there was less distortion and the messages could travel further. Manchester obtained its wireless vans in 1932. Despite some early experiments with personal radios in Brighton in the 1930s, and wider tests in Lancashire in the 1950s, it was not until 1963 that the first practical personal radio sets were tested in Manchester.

In 1965 the Kirkby and later the Accrington system of policing using area constables, detectives and mobile beats, (i.e. radio-equipped vehicles), was introduced. This method of working became known as the 'unit beat' or 'panda car' system when introduced into Manchester in 1968.

Greater Manchester Police now has one of the most modern communications suites ever designed — the Communications and Computer Centre at police headquarters in Chester House, Manchester. It was officially opened by HM the Queen in March 1986 and is one of the largest fully-operational police computer systems in the country. It is designed to efficiently and speedily direct resources in such cases as, for example, a natural disaster or similar major incident. It is used for motorway control, the circulation of information and controls the message switch system (telex) and visual display units, thus speeding up deployment of resources. It can also 'zone' 999 calls to particular areas of the Operations Room for attention by those with the relevant specialised local knowledge. Within the complex is also the computer which operates the criminal records system.

Communications have come a long way from the watchman with his lamp or the early policeman with his rattle to the breath-taking technology of a modern communications and computer centre.

160. *above*: The police wireless station at Manchester Heaton Park in 1938 — the control centre of the Manchester City Police. The scheme was introduced and supervised by Superintendent Aberdein.

161. *below*: The former Control Room at Southmill Street.

162. The present-day communications suite at Chester House Phase II.

163. The communications and computer centre at Chester House.

164a-b. Today visual display unit screens and computer discs are replacing the card indexes and manual files.

TRANSPORT

The earliest form of transport used by the police was, of course, two feet, and from the inception of the modern police in 1829 to the late 1920s this remained the primary means of patrol for forces in all parts of the country. The introduction of mechanisation and the provision of transport occurred gradually with the larger urban forces often developing their own systems independently, while rural forces seemed reluctant to make use of new technology. For example, Cheshire Constabulary in the late nineteenth century still insisted on marching bodies of men to and from destinations, despite the existence of an extensive railway system. The high cost of new equipment discouraged many smaller borough forces who also had to find money for such things as police pay and new premises from carefully-controlled budgets.

165. Condy's Fluid . . . recommended for the feet of policemen — and horses!

Troublesome Feet

Aching, Tender, Tired or Hot Feet are instantly relieved by bathing in water containing a few drops of "Condy's Fluid." All feeling of pain, fatigue or discomfort and every trace of Odour immediately disappear. It imparts a most delicious and lasting sensation of Coolness, Freshness and Purity.

Of all Chemists, 1/-. Insist on having "Condy's Fluid," which contains NO Permanganate of Potash (Poison).

CONDY'S FLUID CO., Goswell Rd., London.

166. *above:* Horse-drawn 'Black-Maria' vehicles were normally used to transport prisoners — here, however, they are being used to transfer 'enemy aliens' to the nearest railway station for deportation.

167. *right:* As well as transferring the injured to hospital, the ambulance litter would also be used for carrying violent or incapable drunks to the police station!

Horse-drawn transport was the rule for all nineteenth century forces although this normally consisted merely of a prison van, or 'Black Maria', and a handful of horse ambulances if that force happened to be responsible for the Ambulance Service as well. A small number of mounted officers were also used, primarily as traffic police, and in the Lancashire Constabulary the Divisional superintendent was provided with a horse to enable him to visit his Divisional stations. In contrast, by the turn of the century, an officer in the Royal Irish Constabulary was expected to provide his own horse-drawn gig as Divisional transport!

The Manchester Police Horse Ambulance

Before Manchester had a police horse ambulance people who were injured or fell sick in a public place were transported to hospital on a litter which was nothing more than a hand-cart.

Manchester's first horse ambulance was donated to the Watch Committee in 1895 by Mr W B Suttle. In February 1896 the horse ambulance was placed with the fire brigade at the Chief Fire Station, Jackson's Row, under the command of the Chief Officer of the brigade, Mr J L Savage. In October 1896 Mr Savage reported on the effectiveness of the horse ambulance. He said that it had been used forty-one times since it had been placed with his Department and that on each occasion a litter would have done just as well. Work for the horse ambulance was of a sporadic nature and it was often impossible to send it out because the men and the horses were engaged at fires. Mr Savage thought that it interfered with the general work of the fire brigade. He said that it impaired their efficiency and he asked the Watch Committee to place it with some other Department. Thus, a year later in 1897, it was placed at the Goulden Street police station in Manchester. The Watch Committee officially handed over control of the Horse Ambulance Service to the police on 10 February 1898 and an ambulance shed was erected at Goulden Street in 1900.

In June 1900 it was decided that police officers should attend St John Ambulance Brigade classes at Newton Street police station in Manchester, the present site of the force museum. Those who passed the Certificate of Proficiency in First Aid were transferred to the Ambulance Corps.

In the same year the Chief Constable, Robert Peacock, thought that if Manchester was to provide an efficient service throughout the city it would be necessary to provide four ambulances, one to be stationed at each police Division. He also suggested that a number of telephone boxes should be placed at different points as a lack of communication would render the system practically useless.

During the First World War, owing to the shortage of men, Boy Scouts had to be used as attendants. It was during this time that the Watch Committee decided to purchase motor ambulances. In 1914 the Royal Army Medical Corps, stationed in Manchester, commandeered four police ambulances and twelve horses for military purposes, so when these were later replaced it was by two motor ambulances costing £723 13s 0d (£723.65) each. The motor ambulance was slowly but surely replacing the horse ambulance as the most common method of transporting patients to hospital.

After the war the number of calls received by the Ambulance Department gradually increased and so did the work performed by the motor ambulances. In 1921 Peacock informed the then head of the Ambulance Department, Inspector Thomas, that more use was to be made of horse ambulances whenever it was possible to keep the horses in

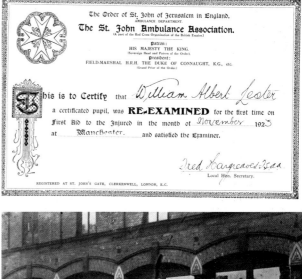

168. *top:* Stretcher drill, probably in the yard of the London Road fire station which was also the site of the force training school. Second from left is PC Arthur Horgan, later to be killed in action in October 1917. All officers are wearing a St John's Ambulance badge on their upper left sleeve.

169. *middle:* The First Aid Certificate. Any officer wishing to gain promotion would need to obtain this first.

170. *bottom:* These motor ambulances were used by the Oldham Borough Police post-First World War.

fit condition in case they were needed by the Mounted Section. The ambulance was to be used whenever possible on all short journeys and for private cases.

By 1928 the Ambulance Service had dropped the word 'Horse' from its title and was known as the Police Ambulance Service. Three years later, in 1931, police ambulances were no longer available for the removal of private cases but were exclusively for taking accident and serious illness cases to hospital. The removal of private cases passed into the hands of the Public Health Department's Ambulance Service.

In 1933 the Minister of Health told local authorities to make agreements for the transporting of patients over district boundaries. At that time it was not uncommon to transfer patients from one ambulance to another when they reached a district boundary although Manchester already had agreements with local district councils. The Police Ambulance Service continued until 1948 when the Government decided that all ambulances were to be transferred to the Local Health Authority.

Motorcycles and Pedal Cycles

Despite its obvious attractions, police forces were not quick to fully adopt the motorcycle as a tool for their day-to-day work, perhaps because the early machines were not reliable or powerful enough. Interestingly, one of the first accounts we have of motorcycle patrol work in this area is from Lancashire where one of the handful of policewomen then employed by the County force was assigned to take out one of the new motorcycles for rural patrol work in the early 1930s.

While pedal cycles for use by beat men and divisional despatch riders had been in general service from the turn of the century, the first purchase of motorcycles in this area seem to have occurred in the mid-1920s. Both Bolton and Rochdale Borough police forces each purchased two AJS motorcycle combinations in 1926. However, the precise role of the machines seems not to have been entirely agreed, for by 1930 Rochdale had replaced both their machines with small motor cars.

The widespread use of motorcycles did not come until the establishment of the police telephone box system in the 1930s. A network of these boxes served each Division connected by telephone to a central Divisional headquarters building. Waiting here was a whole fleet of cars, vans and motorcycles ready to respond to calls for assistance. Some forces decreed that the telephone operators at headquarters had to be trained motor-cyclists so that, if no one else was available, they could respond in an emergency. So it was the motorcycle which remained a vital arm of the box system until the 1960s.

From early days experiments were carried out with on-board wireless equipment but a side-car was usually required to carry the heavy and rather fragile machinery. From the late 1940s a popular motorcycle for police work was the LE Velocette. With its twin-cylinder water-cooled engine and shaft drive it was noted as a quiet reliable performer. One drawback was the radiator and pipes which in the event of an accident could fracture and spill scalding water onto the rider. This bike was used by many forces both in this area and all over the world. In different models and colour schemes it served the police for over twenty years until the late 1960s.

While the Velocette acted as a patrol bike the large 750cc Triumph machine served as a pursuit cycle and was also used to patrol the new motorways which carved their way across the North West in the 1960s. The Triumph, Norton Commando and Velocette were the last British-made motorcycles used in volume by the police; in later years both German and Japanese machines have been used.

With modern high-performance on-board radio equipment, motorcyclists today carry out a wide range of important functions. As well as motorway work they respond to traffic accidents and provide escorts for visiting VIP's. The motorcycle is sometimes the only police vehicle that can reach an incident and will continue to play an important role in the mobile, fast-changing society of today.

171. A group of Manchester dispatch riders from the Edwardian era wearing the regulation 'knickers' and gaiters.

the ideal
lightweight
for police work

Speedometer, ammeter, lights
and ignition switch, are grouped
in panels on the leg-shields

Silent, smooth, safe and amazingly economical,
the 192 c.c. L.E. Velocette is unequalled for
all-round performance and functional good
looks. Car-type transmission, with shaft drive,
gives more mileage with less maintenance.
Standard equipment includes twin panniers and
luxury weather protection.

Starting is by hand lever,
requiring only light effort even
for a cold start. A carburettor
starting choke is provided.

the *SILENT*

Velocette

Generousmudguarding,together
with legshields and two-level
footboards, afford excellent
weather protection. Dual seat
can be provided as an extra.

*Full details of the L.E.
will be sent by return
to interested authorities and consultation will be readily
arranged.*

MODEL L.E.

VELOCE LTD., YORK ROAD, BIRMINGHAM 28.

172. *top:* Salford City Police Mobile Section at the Crescent police
station in 1937.

173. *above:* The Velocette machine was given wide publicity in
police publications as shown in this 1950s Police College magazine
advertisement.

174. *top right:* Escorting wide loads is one of the many duties the
modern police motorcyclists undertake.

Motor Vans and Cars

The introduction of motorisation occurred in the police
service at the beginning of the twentieth century. The
Metropolitan Police appear to have taken a lead and indeed
to have tried initially to set standards for police motor
vehicles, and in the 1920s designed a standard utility van
for police work.

Motor cars were first used by the Metropolitan Police in
1903. Two Wolseleys were purchased at a cost of £550 each.
At the time there was considerable doubt as to whether
these cars, designed for use by the Commissioner, Assistant
Commissioner and superintendents, could be fully utilised
and their purchase justified. An Engineering Branch was
formed by 1919 to develop new vehicles and adapt standard
models.

In 1920 London police were using thirty cars but by
1929 the number had risen to 220 cars with some
Departments, such as the Flying Squad, using vehicles
fitted with a concealed wireless.

In the late 1920s a design for a general utility van was
conceived by the Engineering Branch of the Metropolitan
Police. It was designed to act as a mobile back-up to the
recently-introduced police telephone box system. An
emergency phone call from police or public was received at
a Divisional switch-board and a mobile response was made
by one of the vehicle fleet. The utility van was designed to be
used as a personnel transporter, a means of moving arrested
persons from the scene of the arrest, a breakdown recovery
van or an ambulance.

In addition, in the 1920s a prison motor van was also
introduced to replace the earlier heavy motor van carrying
twelve prisoners which in turn replaced the horse-drawn
'Black Maria' of the nineteenth century. Built in the same
way as a motor coach, it had an entrance at the front and
passengers sat facing the driver. In the old horse-drawn

175. Mr Norman Redfern, General Manager of Parkers in Bradshawgate, handing over Bolton's first police sports car in 1935.

176. *above:* Two members of the Manchester Police Transport Section pose alongside open-topped Alvis sports cars which were popular in many forces.

van, prisoners were placed in little cubicles to either side of a central gangway and sat sideways-on sometimes with two or three people crammed into a space designed for one. The stuffy cramped conditions often induced motion sickness.

The great boost to provincial motorisation came with the adoption of the telephone box system and with it the attendant vans and motorcycles.

The typical police car of the late 1920s and early 1930s was a heavy vehicle sometimes fitted with a fire-bell at the front and a police sign on the roof. Often capable of 75 mph they could accelerate from 10mph to 60mph in fifteen seconds.

In the later 1930s, many forces experimented with lighter vehicles capable of catching the 'motor bandits' who were seen as posing a major threat to law and order. Criminals driving fast cars were carrying out robberies, sometimes armed, and then fleeing the scene in moments. It is probable that the danger posed by these 'robbery teams' was exaggerated but Lancashire Constabulary purchased a small number of Lagonda sports cars, while in 1935 Bolton Borough took delivery of a sports car, built by the Swallow Coach Building Company, which was later to become the Jaguar.

Lancashire was to acquire a reputation in later decades as being in the fore-front of vehicle use and by the 1960s, when the first motorways were introduced in their area, the force adopted Triumph sports cars in order not to be left behind the faster-moving traffic. Zephyr estate cars were also introduced by Lancashire which were converted to carry a full range of equipment to be used at the scene of an accident.

177. *left:* The typical equipment load for a Zephyr motorway police vehicle would include signs, cones, oil lamps, a pedometer, crow bars, first-aid kit and a dustpan and brush.

In the 1950s and 1960s Triumph motor cars, together with Wolseleys and Jaguars, were used by most forces, initially still fitted with a bell but later with a siren. Austin Morris radio vans were a common sight in the late 1950s and early 1960s whilst another Austin, the Morris 1000, was used in Lancashire in the experimental system that was later to be known as the 'panda car' or 'unit beat' system, introduced in 1968.

Currently a variety of vehicles are used by police but the dream of the Metropolitan Police Engineering Branch in the 1920s, of producing a standard range of vehicles for the police, has still not been achieved, commercial vehicles converted to police use having varying degrees of success.

Ford, the Rover Group, Peugeot, General Motors and Bedford all supply vehicles for police use with specialist firms providing purpose-built bodies and fittings.

The Motorway Group

The Greater Manchester Police's Motorway Group is based at the Granada service area at Birch on the M62 eastbound. This Group polices the M56, M58, M6, M61, M62, M63, M602, M66, A627(M) and A6144(M) motorways which carry over three-quarters of a million vehicles daily. The Group is commanded by a superintendent. Since the inception of Greater Manchester Police in 1974 the motorways have increased in size and have undergone many major schemes to extend them.

Many incidents and accidents occur on the motorways daily and in the past, single accidents involving over one hundred vehicles have occurred.

The M62 provides a vital link between the east and west coasts of England and is a major transport route for trade and industry on both sides of the Pennines. The road reaches a height of 1,256ft above sea-level at junction twenty-two (Rockingstones) which is reached, after a considerable climb of approximately twelve and a half miles in length, when travelling eastbound from Birch service area. The motorway is believed to be the highest in Europe.

In January 1979 the M62 motorway between Birch service area and into West Yorkshire beyond junction twenty-two was closed for three days because of arctic weather conditions. This resulted in over six hundred vehicles being trapped between junction twenty-one (Milnrow) and junction twenty-two. Snow-drifts quickly piled up and, in some cases, vehicles were completely covered by snow. During this time the motorway police, together with the other emergency services such as fire, ambulance and maintenance crews, were fully extended for three days in rescuing several hundreds of motorists. Through the good hospitality of Granada Services the rescued motorists were taken down to the service area and provided with hot drinks and blankets as they were stranded for up to twenty-four hours at a time. At one point the service area resembled a war-time evacuation centre.

The work of the Motorway Group was recognised in a unique way by the Automobile Association. On 21 May 1980 Viscount D L'Isle, VC, KG, KCMG, KCVO, then Vice-President of the Association, presented a silver medal of the Association to the Chief Constable at a ceremony at the Savoy Hotel in London. This was the first occasion at which the silver medal had been presented to any person or group within any police area.

In January 1987 the efforts of the Motorway Group and maintenance crews were overcome and again the M62 motorway was closed. On yet another occasion Granada's service area provided accommodation for several hundred

178. *top:* An impressive line-up of Lancashire police vehicles. Note the use of roof numerals to aid identification by helicopter.

179. *middle:* The Morris 1000 was among the first police vehicles to bear the characteristic blue and white 'panda' colour scheme.

180. *bottom:* Students at the Force Driving School in the 1960s study a 'skeletonised' MG sports car.

181. A selection of the 1,000-plus vehicles currently in the GMP fleet.

rescued motorists until such time as the motorway was re-opened within twenty-four hours.

Although the motorway has only closed on two occasions there have been many other times during the winter months when it has been severely affected by adverse weather conditions but the efforts of the emergency services have kept the traffic moving and prevented further closures.

One of the major problems confronting the Motorway Group police and motorists has been the proliferation of roadworks on the motorways. Due to the volume of traffic using them much repair work has been absolutely essential, together with the extension of the motorway network. Major building programmes have taken place for the more heavily-used motorways such as the M62 and the M63. The M63 over Barton high-level bridge once consisted of two lanes and, in some places, no hard shoulder. The widening of this motorway between junction one (Eccles) and junction seven (Stretford) was absolutely essential. A three-year programme commenced in early spring 1986 to increase the carriageway from two lanes to three and a hard shoulder. Likewise, on the M62 between junction twenty-one (Milnrow) and junction twenty-two (Rockingstones), a crawler lane eastbound to cater for heavy vehicles was also considered essential and this was completed by the end of 1988.

It was recognised that, although there were three lanes of carriageway on the M62, the sheer volume of traffic necessitated that an additional lane was required and consideration was given to a programme to widen the motorway. In addition it was found necessary to up-date and modernise its lighting and signalling systems and at the time of printing, this work was in progress with the building of additional gantries and signals.

Many of the other motorways within the network have constantly needed maintenance and repair work causing much inconvenience to the motorist. The police have sympathised with the public who, in general, have accepted the various inconveniences in the hope that, at the end of the day, travelling on the motorways will be safer and less time-consuming.

182. The scene at Birch motorway service area on the M62 in mid-January 1987 when many motorists and truck drivers had to abandon their vehicles.

MOUNTED AND DOG SECTIONS

Mounted

The forerunner of today's Mounted Police Section was London's Bow Street horse patrol which was set up by Sir Richard Ford in 1805. Nicknamed the 'Robin Redbreasts' due to their distinctive red waistcoats, the horse patrol, comprising ex-Cavalry men, was designed to combat the menace of highwaymen and numbered fifty-four strong.

After Sir Robert Peel's Metropolitan Police Act of 1829, the Bow Street horse patrol was placed under the new police office at Scotland Yard and became known as the mounted police. Outside London mounted policing was not so advanced and usually consisted of members of the public banding together to pursue felons. By 1839 five hundred such groups were formed, many of which used horses.

Until the advent of the motor car and its subsequent introduction into the police service, horses were the main mode of transport. In 1900 the Chief Constable of Manchester, Robert Peacock, submitted a report to the Watch Committee arguing that mounted police were needed. A force of fifty was suggested using existing officers in the force with experience of horses. The Watch Committee rejected the idea of using fifty men but agreed to a Mounted Section of twenty-five which was raised to forty the following year. When necessary these were supplemented by horses borrowed from Hulme Barracks or the Police Horse Ambulance Department.

In June 1915 mounted patrols by Special Constables were introduced to make up for the deficiency in the numbers of the regular officers in the Mounted Section having joined the Military Police for war duties.

One of the main duties of the mounted patrols was the supervision of traffic. The Manchester Police Mounted Section was originally supervised by the inspector of the Ambulance Department but, due to his increased workload, the Mounted Section received its own inspector in May 1921.

The following year concern was raised over the frequent use of the motor ambulance as it was feared the horses would become unfit for use in the Mounted Section but it later became evident that the fears were unfounded as motor vehicles and horses could be fully integrated into police work.

In the 1920s and 1930s the cost of a single horse was £75 and it was a condition of the sale that the horses had a trial period of six months in which they could be replaced if found to be nervous or physically unfit.

By 1954 there were only nineteen horses left in the Manchester Police force. This was due to the stringent financial situation after the war, the diminished need for the Mounted Section to control traffic and the fact that motor vehicles began to play a vital role in policing the area as well as being cheaper to maintain. However, after the 1974 amalgamation, those outer areas which had their own Mounted Sections incorporated them into the strength of the new force and by 1980 the total number of horses had increased to forty.

During the 1970s the Mounted Section became better funded and in 1976 they moved to prestigious new stables at Hough End Centre in Chorlton. Four horses were kept at Bury and Leigh Divisions with facilities being made available at Stretford police station to be used when covering football matches at nearby Manchester United.

Despite the high technology used in police work the Mounted Section still play an important role in operational policing, especially in football crowds and riot control. The mounted officer has the advantage of height for observation

183. *top:* A police inspection of mounted Special Constabulary officers during the period of the Great War.

184. A Salford Borough Police mounted officer circa 1913.

185. *top left:* The Mounted Section's stables, Moss Side, in 1972 before they moved to their prestigious new premises at Hough End four years later.

186. *middle left:* Apart from extensive training facilities for GMP's Mounted and Dog Sections the Hough End complex also houses the central Sports and Social Club.

187. *bottom left:* Public order uniform worn by the Mounted Branch in crowd-control situations. At such times protective eye shields are also put onto the horses' tack.

188. *top:* Officers wearing ceremonial uniform for such occasions as Royal visits and civic events.

189. *above:* All in a day's work . . . GMP's horses enter into the spirit of the force Families' Day in 1986.

which is particularly useful when searching for missing people in difficult terrain. Mounted Section officers have a specialist knowledge of animals and are often called upon to assist, for example, when an animal is found wandering on the road.

Apart from their operational work the Mounted Section carry out escort and ceremonial work as well as entering competitions and participating in displays and shows throughout the UK as well as the Greater Manchester area.

Dogs

The history of Dog Sections goes back to Roman times. Every legion had its Dog Section whose purpose was to search and track escaped prisoners and runaway slaves, using training methods similar to those of today.

Police dogs are of two types — executive and criminal tracking. The executive dog is used to chase and apprehend criminals, deter attacks on police officers and has been used at night when its superior senses help the constable on the beat. The breeds which have been considered for use in this role are Collies, Retrievers, Bulldogs, Airedales and Sheepdogs but in present times the most frequently used is the German Shepherd (Alsatian). The criminal tracking dog is used to chase criminals by following a trail and the original British dog used to carry out this work was the Bloodhound.

In the early 1900s Britain used tracking dogs more than executives. At that time Major E H Richardson had written a book called *War, Police and Watchdogs* extolling the virtues of dogs to Chief Constables all over the country. Many forces began to use his dogs — for a fee — and it is recorded that his Bloodhounds 'traced' the murderers of a Mrs Laurd.

Many Chief Constables were unconvinced of the value of dogs and in 1908 a police inspector, Captain H D Terry, found them to be "of very little value". In a letter to another inspector, J J Eden, he particularly noted that a prisoner had escaped from Winchester prison and the dogs under "every favourable condition" could not follow the trail. Captain T J Smith, Chief Constable of Cheshire Constabulary, forbade his constables on night duty from being accompanied on their beats by dogs because of "the partiality of the rural policeman for dogs which could catch rabbits"!

Despite setbacks and antagonism there was a Police Dogs' Training Centre at Harrow-on-the-Hill in the north-west region of the London Police District in 1910, and between 1910 and 1920 many forces contemplated setting up a Dog Section. The Chief Constables of Birkenhead and Bradford suggested the purchase of dogs in 1910 and 1914 but it was not until the late 1950s that they were actually bought.

The Bolton Police force bought a dog in 1914 to help in policing a Miners' Strike. The Alsatian named Royal was to have been the first of four dogs but no others were bought and Royal died in 1918. The Cheshire Constabulary kept one Bloodhound in 1920 at 4d (2p) a day but this died of distemper after nine months and was not replaced.

During the 1914-1918 war the Germans used dogs previously unseen in Great Britain for guarding installations and for use as messengers. The dogs were German Shepherds, noted for intelligence, adaptability and stamina. Gradually these were introduced into this country although the more popular name of Alsatian was adopted.

In the 1950s experiments were made by the London Metropolitan Police into the use that could be made of dogs, and several breeds were tested. Bloodhounds, Labradors and Dobermans were amongst those considered but the

190. The rural policeman and his trusty dog — gamekeeper turned poacher?

191A. *bottom:* The General Order outlining the introduction of police dogs in Manchester.

191B. The first four officers trained as dog handlers with Manchester City Police were:

Bill Hughes   Gordon Stewart
Fred Lee   Bob Burton

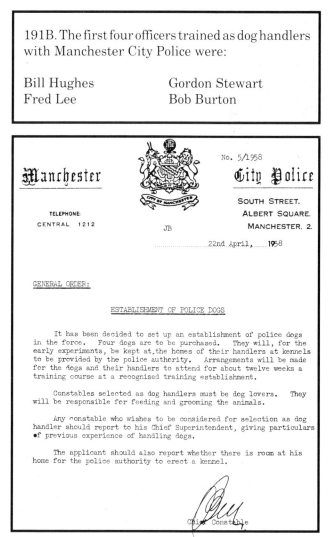

Manchester   City Police

No. 5/1958

TELEPHONE:
CENTRAL 1212   JB

SOUTH STREET,
ALBERT SQUARE,
MANCHESTER. 2.

22nd April, 1958

GENERAL ORDER:

ESTABLISHMENT OF POLICE DOGS

It has been decided to set up an establishment of police dogs in the force. Four dogs are to be purchased. They will, for the early experiments, be kept at the homes of their handlers at kennels to be provided by the police authority. Arrangements will be made for the dogs and their handlers to attend for about twelve weeks a training course at a recognised training establishment.

Constables selected as dog handlers must be dog lovers. They will be responsible for feeding and grooming the animals.

Any constable who wishes to be considered for selection as dog handler should report to his Chief Superintendent, giving particulars of previous experience of handling dogs.

The applicant should also report whether there is room at his home for the police authority to erect a kennel.

Chief Constable

Alsatians proved to be the most effective. It was not until the 1950s that many forces established a permanent Dog Section.

In March 1958 the Watch Committee recommended that a Manchester City Police Dog Section be established and in 1959 PC's William Hughes and Gordon Stewart were appointed the city's first police dog handlers. With Alsatians Kim and Rinty they attended Birmingham Police Dog Training Centre. During 1959 the number of dogs rose to eight — two for each division — and they were trained in Birmingham and Lancashire but by 1966 Manchester had obtained its own training facilities.

As today, most of the early dogs were donations from the public and were kept at the handlers' homes. Later, following the example of other forces, central police kennels were built in Brownley Road, Wythenshawe, which would look after sick animals or those whose handlers were temporarily away from home. In 1968 the kennels were moved to Oakwood Park in Salford because of the better training facilities.

In 1969 two Labrador tracking dogs were purchased for the Manchester Dog Section and were specially trained to detect the drug cannabis and search for explosives.

In 1976 the Dog Section was moved to the new Hough End Centre although the majority of GMP's 120 dogs continue to live at home with their handlers. The complex is the training centre for dogs and their handlers in GMP. In the same year two policewomen became dog handlers within the force.

Today, police dogs are invaluable in operational work as well as participating in shows and competitions for the enjoyment of members of the public, young and old.

194. An aircraft search in progress by a highly-trained Labrador.

192. *above:* Her Majesty's Inspector of Constabulary visiting the Salford Dog Section in the 1960s.
193. The GMP Dog Display Team in 1985 under the control of ex-Chief Inspector Don Featonby.

195. *above:* PW Janice Rudkin, GMP's first policewoman dog handler, joined the Section in May 1976.
196. Searching open ground above Saddleworth during the recent Moors Murders enquiry.

TRAINING

Constables

In the earliest days of the police force, very little thought was given to the training of new constables. All that was demanded of the men was that they be physically fit and of a given height, normally 5ft 9ins, although this latter requirement could be waived if there were difficulties in recruiting sufficient officers.

The method used to train recruits in the early days appears to have been to place a new constable in the company of a more experienced one and let him give instruction in the duties and activities of a policeman. This practise is still carried out today by officers known as 'Tutor Constables'. Also it seems likely that copies of local byelaws and Government statutes were available for the recruit to study but, in view of the fact that many could not read and write properly, it is doubtful that much 'book learning' study was undertaken in those early days.

The men themselves were subject to a very strict, military discipline. Primary emphasis was placed on the supervisory officers knowing what the constable was doing and where he was on patrol. Therefore the men were told to walk their beats in a set direction, proceeding from one 'point' to another (a point being a recognisable place, perhaps at a street corner, where the sergeant could meet the constable and information could be exchanged). In addition, the constable was to march around the beat with a measured pace so that his location could be accurately surmised by the sergeant.

Little was expected of the constable for it was assumed that he was only likely to serve between six months and three years and so was not inclined to gain initiative through experience but rather would require constant supervision like some mill-hand or regular soldier.

Indeed, the poor attitude of the Police Authorities, coupled with the low pay, the few chances for reward or promotion and bad working conditions, meant that most constables did actually resign after only a few months' duty.

In the later nineteenth century it was becoming clear that a changing society, and in the cities a more sophisticated population, was in turn demanding more of the police and placing a greater onus on the individual officers to deal on the spot with sometimes delicate or potentially violent situations.

Thus the Salford Police Instruction Book of 1886 clearly stated that the main duties of the constable were "the prevention of crime, the detection of offenders and the preservation of the peace". It also laid down the method of foot patrol — outside of the footpath by day so as to be a visible deterrent but next to the houses at night so as to be able to watch for burglars unobserved.

The book informed constables that they would be required to pay at least one penny a month to the band fund and that they should take pains to remove orange peel from highways wherever this potential hazard should occur. The handbook also gives an insight into other unofficial practises that were being carried out. The book stated that the activity called 'knocking-up' — awakening factory workers in the early morning either by a call from the street or a pole tapped on the bedroom window — was strictly forbidden. Due to the strict ban, one may assume that this practise was wide-spread, particularly as the 'knocker-up' received a small remuneration.

A major step forward in training was taken in 1899 in Manchester where the newly-appointed Chief Constable, Robert Peacock, decided to press for separate education classes for police officers in order to improve their level of

197. *top:* An unchanging aspect of police routine is parading-on before commencing a tour of duty as depicted in this turn of the century photograph.

198. *middle:* Contrary to the majority of his fellow officers, Inspector Frederick Holland of the Manchester Police served for 33 years. Shown here is his leaving certificate.

199. *bottom:* The attendance card produced at police evening classes which would be date-stamped on the reverse after each lecture.

general education and to pave the way for a better-equipped, career-orientated force.

At the opening session held in the Lord Mayor's parlour at the town hall in Manchester on 15 September 1899, the Chief Constable remarked that before this occasion no special classes had been arranged for the benefit of the force and went on: "It would not be advisable, in the interests of the force, for constables to attend classes where they would be compelled to associate with persons with whom they would frequently come into contact when on duty in the streets, as the less close the association between civilians and constables the better it is for the force."

The Manchester School Board arranged for classes to be held solely for police officers and wherever possible on police premises, attendance being required three nights a week. It was felt that the 'older generation', denied the benefits of the School Board twenty or thirty years ago, must educate themselves in order to compete or hold their own against their contemporaries. The Chief Constable stated that: "In the police force . . . education is absolutely essential if a man is to perform his duty satisfactorily to himself and to the public". The instruction in police duty was to be given by the Chief Constable in person and to that end he composed a series of lectures which were each followed by a question and answer session. The presentations were given once a fortnight and ran from 15 September to 22 December 1899. Peacock remarked: "I should like to impress upon you most forcibly that these classes are established for your own benefit and not for mine . . . I could certainly employ my time in other work . . . but I am anxious to see that every man in the Manchester City Police force attains such a degree of education that he will be qualified to at once take any position in the police service that may become vacant . . . I am looking forward to a time in the near future when every man will be able to write, compose and properly complete his own reports." As an incentive he added: "In the near future promotion will be made solely by examination."

At the outset of the classes 260 officers had declared an interest in participating. The topics of the lectures given over those months mainly covered the licensing, gaming and betting laws but also public health, highways and transport. Local Acts peculiar to Manchester which conferred special powers or responsibilities were also studied.

By the 1930s the system of education classes, some of which were held at the Newton Street police station, had developed into a fully-operational training school. This not only trained Manchester officers but took in trainee constables from the surrounding borough forces whose local authorities were unable or unwilling to afford the considerable costs of a proper training establishment. The

200-201. Intensive study in subjects such as shorthand (*above right*), law and police procedures led to examinations to gauge candidates' fitness for duty and future promotion.

site of the school was on London Road at the fire brigade and police complex which also housed the Coroner's Court. A surviving training manual shows that in 1938 basic training lasted thirteen weeks.

On the first week Manchester recruits reported to the Chief Constable's office at Southmill Street on the Wednesday at 9.00 am and then proceeded to the training school. Outside recruits went directly to the school and arranged lodgings. In the afternoon books and kit were issued and the rules of the school were explained. The first full week of training commenced on Monday morning with physical training, a lecture on legal principles with swimming and life-saving drill in the afternoon. The lectures continued all week with a visit to the police courts at Minshull Street on Friday. An oral examination on Saturday completed the week's packed schedule.

202. *right:* Apart from his educational reforms Chief Constable Peacock reorganised the scale of pay and allowances as seen here from the 1923 Instruction Book.

203. *below*: The first Senior Course held at Bruche in 1952 included officers from Wigan, Stockport, Oldham, Cheshire, Lancashire and Bolton.

Pay and Allowances.

1. The following is the authorised Scale of Pay and Allowances applicable to all members of the Force:—

RANK.	Salaries and Pay.	Contributions to Pensions Fund, at Rate of 2½% of Pay.
SUPERINTENDENTS.		
5th Class (on appointment)	£450 per annum.	£11 5s. per annum.
4th Class (after 1 year)	£470 ,,	£11 15s. ,,
3rd Class (after 2 years)	£490 ,,	£12 5s. ,,
2nd Class (after 3 years)	£510 ,,	£12 15s. ,,
1st Class (after 4 years)	£530 ,,	£13 5s. ,,
CHIEF INSPECTORS.		
5th Class (on appointment)	143/10 per week.	3s. 7d. per week.
4th Class (after 1 year)	147/8 ,,	3s. 8d. ,,
3rd Class (after 2 years)	151/6 ,,	3s. 9d. ,,
2nd Class (after 3 years)	155/4 ,,	3s. 10d. ,,
1st Class (after 4 years)	159/2 ,,	3s. 11d. ,,
INSPECTORS.		
5th Class (on appointment)	122/9 ,,	3s. 0d. ,,
4th Class (after 1 year)	126/7 ,,	3s. 1d. ,,
3rd Class (after 2 years)	130/5 ,,	3s. 3d. ,,
2nd Class (after 3 years)	134/3 ,,	3s. 4d. ,,
1st Class (after 4 years)	138/1 ,,	3s. 5d. ,,
SERGEANTS.		
6th Class (on appointment)	100/- ,,	2s. 6d. ,,
5th Class (after 1 year)	102/6 ,,	2s. 6d. ,,
4th Class (after 2 years)	105/- ,,	2s. 7d. ,,
3rd Class (after 3 years)	107/6 ,,	2s. 8d. ,,
2nd Class (after 4 years)	110/- ,,	2s. 9d. ,,
1st Class (after 5 years)	112/6 ,,	2s. 9d. ,,
CONSTABLES.		
11th Class (on appointment, on probation)	70/- ,,	1s. 9d. ,,
10th Class (after 1 year, or on termination of Probationary Period if this is extended)	72/- ,,	1s. 9d. ,,
9th Class (after 2 yrs' from appointment)	74/- ,,	1s. 10d. ,,
8th Class (after 3 yrs' from appointment)	76/- ,,	1s. 10d. ,,
7th Class (after 4 yrs' from appointment)	78/- ,,	1s. 11d. ,,
6th Class (after 5 yrs' from appointment)	80/- ,,	2s. 0d. ,,
5th Class (after 6 yrs' from appointment)	82/- ,,	2s. 0d. ,,
4th Class (after 7 yrs' from appointment)	84/- ,,	2s. 1d. ,,
3rd Class (after 8 yrs' from appointment)	86/- ,,	2s. 1d. ,,
2nd Class (after 9 yrs' from appointment)	88/- ,,	2s. 2d. ,,
1st Class after 10 yrs' from appointment	90/- ,,	2s. 3d. ,,
1st Good Conduct Class (after 17 years)	92/6 ,,	2s. 3d. ,,
2nd Good Conduct Class (after 22 years) (Granted for Good Conduct and Efficiency, and subject to the Chief Constable's discretion.)	95/- ,,	2s. 4d. ,,

204a-b. *left:* These 1930s photographs show the range of training undertaken from traffic laws to wireless technology.

205. *right:* Despite the many posters to attract recruits, Manchester Police struggled to maintain full strength throughout the 1950s. Excellent career prospects could not entice people away from better-paid and safer work in industry.

During the training period three trips were made to the city police courts and visits were also made to the city quarter sessions and the Manchester Assizes then situated at the old Victorian complex near Strangeways. Later a trip was made to the Criminal Records Office at police headquarters in Southmill Street.

A final oral examination and assessment report completed the initial training. Throughout the weeks one day, usually Saturday, was spent working a beat in the company of an experienced constable.

To assist the police in their duties and report writing, various booklets were privately published by Police Associations. One such was *Police Duty, Catechism and Reports* by H Childs, published by the International Christian Police Association. Available for many years from the 1900s to the 1930s it gave standard forms for reports on every conceivable subject. Topics covered in the fifteenth edition of 1928 included 'Attempted murder', 'Burglar in house', 'Horse ill in street', 'Horse running away, doing damage', 'Stolen dogs', 'Man shot by gamekeeper', and 'Washing clothing in public drinking fountain'.

A similar publication was Howard Vincent's *Police Code* which commenced publication in the 1890s and continued through many editions long after the author's death at the turn of the century. The Code set out the duties and responsibilities of the constable alphabetically and also set out the standard form for a reward bill, and various types of warrants. The popularity of these books suggest that, in smaller forces at least, very few handbooks and instruction manuals were provided for the officers to use.

After the Second World War, the training of officers in the Manchester area took on a new development with the opening of the regional training centre at Bruche near Warrington. It acted as the centre for the No 1 Region, of which the Greater Manchester area was later to form the central part. The school was provided by the Home Office and managed by a committee representing the Police Authorities in the catchment areas.

The need for higher level, academic and management-style courses for senior officers had been felt necessary for many years and this was at last catered for in 1948 by the establishment of the Police National College at Ryton-on-Dunsmore in Warwickshire. The college moved to its present location at Bramshill House, near Basingstoke, in 1960.

The growing sophistication of criminals, together with the post-war crime wave and the shortfall in recruits, meant that more and more was being expected of the new constable and every effort was taken to ensure that an unsuitable candidate was 'weeded out' of the intake before too much valuable effort and money had been wasted. In 1955 in Manchester more officers were lost through wastage than were recruited in a force already under strength.

Training, of course, continued on a local force level. Although many forces started their own schools, Manchester still acted as regional centre for initial training. In the 1960s officers from Oldham, Stockport and even Cumberland attended the school which, by 1962, had moved to Longsight Divisional headquarters in the south of the city. By 1975, soon after the formation of Greater Manchester Police, training was transferred to Peterloo House in Dickinson Street in central Manchester. Conditions at Peterloo House

were, however, very cramped as the building was shared with various other police Departments. In 1977 therefore, arrangements were made for accommodation to be provided at a teacher training college in Sedgley Park, Prestwich. The use of Sedgley Park proved a great success as residential training was made possible. The Chief Constable's Report for 1977 highlighted this and commented: "When the need to travel was not a consideration . . . the training day was greatly increased. In addition students, free from worrying about rush-hour travel, were more easily attuned to study".

In 1979 it became possible for the whole training school to move to Sedgley Park and it has developed from that time into a centre providing not only traditional basic training courses but also the sophisticated and specialist courses demanded by the needs and problems of present-day society. Great emphasis is still placed, however, on the role of the 'Tutor Constable' who by example and practical demonstration imparts the rudiments of good police work to the recruit.

Cadets

The establishment of the Cadet Corps in police forces was primarily a response to the difficulties experienced by the police in attracting and keeping recruits in the years following the Second World War.

There had in fact been a precedent set for the

QUALIFYING EXAMINATIONS

POLICE SUBJECTS

APRIL 14th, 1954.

CONSTABLE TO SERGEANT.

CRIMINAL LAW.

Answer All Questions

1. "A," "B" and "C" agree together to steal certain valuable jewellery from the house of "X".

   During the night "A" and "B" go to "X's" house where "A" forces open a door and enters, while "B" remains outside to keep guard. "X" hears the noise, and overpowers "A" before he has found the jewellery. "B" runs away and telephones to "C" who has remained at the headquarters of the gang.

   "C" then takes a car which he finds unattended in the street and drives to the aid of "B". Whilst he is driving at 70 miles an hour down a narrow road without headlights he runs over a pedestrian and kills him.

   Draw up the charge or charges against "A", "B" and "C" jointly or severally, as you think proper. (25)

2. Consider the following cases and indicate what offences (if any) have been committed :—

   (a) "A" was employed as an engineer at a garage, above which was a flat occupied by the garage attendant. One day as "A" was leaving the garage he lit a cigarette and thoughtlessly threw the match down near the entrance to the garage, where petrol was lying on the floor. A fire started and the caretaker, who was in the flat above, was trapped in the fire and burned to death.

   (b) "B" entered "C's" house for the purpose of committing a robbery. When he had opened "C's" safe his torch went out so he struck a match and accidentally set fire to the house. The occupants died as a consequence. (15)

3. (a) Give a definition of a "false pretence".
   (b) Write out a charge for this offence. (10)

EVIDENCE AND PROCEDURE IN CRIMINAL COURTS.

Answer All Questions

1. Comment upon the following :—

   (a) Circumstantial evidence.
   (b) Evidence of Accomplice.
   (c) Evidence of handwriting.
   (d) Leading questions. (20)

2. Outline the nature of the offence of "Receiving", and indicate any particular rules of evidence applicable to the offence. (10)

3. What must the prosecution prove in a charge of :—

   (a) Bigamy.
   (b) Incest ? (15)

QUALIFYING EXAMINATIONS

EDUCATIONAL SUBJECTS.

APRIL 13th, 1954.

SERGEANT TO INSPECTOR.

SECTION A.

WRITING

including handwriting, spelling, punctuation and the writing and composition of reports.

All Questions to be Answered

1. Write a composition on one of the following subjects :—
   (a) The detective in fiction.
   (b) The use of leisure.
   (c) The influence of newspapers.
   (d) The United Nations. (75)

2. Write a short report of not more than 150 words about a street accident to a pedestrian (not involving a vehicle). (25)

SECTION B.

ARITHMETIC

All Questions to be Answered

1. $$\dfrac{5\frac{3}{8} - 2\frac{5}{8}}{4\frac{1}{8} \text{ of } 1\frac{7}{8}}$$ (10)

2. Out of a cask of wine, of which a sixth part had leaked away, 9 gallons were drawn, and then the cask was two-thirds full. How much did it hold ? (15)

3. Express £2 16s. 6d. as the decimal of £1. (10)

4. A tradesman sells an article at a price one-fourth greater than the price at which he bought it. If he sold it at 3s. 3d. per lb., how much did it cost him per cwt ? (15)

5. "A" gets 2s. 6d. for every shilling which "B" gets, and "B" gets four times as much as "C" ; between them they get £4 15s. 7½d. What does each person get ? (15)

6. Rain injures 6¼ per cent. of a truckload of corn weighing 4 tons 9 cwts. 1 qr. 4 lbs. What is the weight of the damaged grain ? (10)

7. A man has a yearly income of £600. He saves one-sixth of it, pays 15 per cent. of the remainder in rent and taxes, and spends the rest. How much does he spend, excluding rent and taxes ? (15

8. If 2,000 articles are retailed at 7½d. each, and a profit of £12 10s. is made on the whole, find the wholesale price of each. (10)

206a-b. *left:* Two examples of typical examination papers for the mid-1950s designed to test the all-round ability of the candidate.

207a-c. *opposite (bottom), top right and centre:* The Cadet Initial Course in August 1967. It was hoped that physical training, education and practical work experience would prepare many of them for life in the regular force.

208. *bottom right:* The Chief Constable and ex-Chief Superintendent Charles Abraham inspecting the GMP Cadet Corps shortly before its disbandment.

employment of teenagers by the police during the last war. Police messengers were boys who were provided with uniforms and bicycles and formed a communication network between police stations. Bombing often disrupted telephone lines and during raids messengers carried vital information about damage and casualties.

Faced with rising crime, poor housing and pay scales which had fallen behind other workers, police forces of the late 1940s and early 1950s struggled to keep up to strength. In order to create a 'pool' of young people already enthusiastic about police work it was decided in Manchester to instigate a Cadet Scheme and the first twelve cadets were enrolled on 7 January 1953. Following a basic training course, the twelve were placed in various headquarters Departments. The scheme was an immediate success. Numbers increased and by 1956 fifty cadets were being recruited. While progression to the regular force was not seen as automatic, it was strongly hoped that an introduction to police work, together with good sporting opportunities, would persuade many to join. The Government helped this by permitting cadets to defer their period of National Service thus making a transfer to the force simpler.

In the 1960s cadet training was carried out at Longsight police station and the recruits underwent an initial six or seven week course which covered subjects such as physical training, swimming, orienteering and, whilst law was not on the syllabus, it was possible, by teaching the principles of law, to give cadets an impression of regular police training. After an examination and a passing-out parade the cadets were seconded to police departments or increasingly to outside bodies such as hospitals and old people's homes. Cadets had to be between sixteen and eighteen years of age to join, the upper limit being the minimum age that the Police Training Centre at Bruche would accept a regular recruit.

The Cadet Scheme was generally successful in its aims and the cadets themselves put in many hours of hard work serving the community at large. By the 1970s and early 1980s however, the justification in maintaining cadets had declined. Increases in pay awarded by Edmund Davies, coupled with the increased difficulty in finding employment, meant that recruitment to the regular police increased. Finally in June 1985, because of financial implications, the Greater Manchester Police decided to discontinue its Cadet Corps, ending a useful and interesting period which had provided a source of recruits, a number of whom are the Chief Officers of today.

THE SPECIAL CONSTABULARY.

The place of the Special Constable is a long and honorable one in the annals of police history. From time immemorial, ordinary citizens have been called upon to assist the regular forces of law and order.

Traditionally, the constable of a town or village in the days before Robert Peel's police force swore-in fellow citizens should a situation arise that he alone could not handle, such as on market day or at times of public unrest.

At the 1819 Peterloo Massacre in Manchester, the then deputy constable of the town, Joseph Nadin, had enrolled under him a force of about three hundred Specials to try and police the meeting of some 60,000 in Petersfields. Indeed, one of the eleven killed on that tragic day was a Special Constable named John Ashworth.

The earliest legislation relating to Specials was the Special Constables' Act of 1831. This officially gave the Chief Police Officer of a district the power to appoint Special Constables on a temporary basis as a result of specific occurrences. Thus in the 1840s during the time of the protest marches and demonstrations of the political reformers known as Chartists, many thousands of Specials were enrolled.

In the aftermath of the murder of Sergeant Brett of the Manchester Police in 1867, Specials joined the regular police and troops who lined the streets of Salford during the execution of the three Irishmen convicted of his murder.

During the First World War, the national emergency and the recall of many regular police officers to their regiments led Chief Constables to enrol many Specials. The Special Constables' Act 1914 was passed allowing the Chief Officer of Police to appoint Specials even though "a tumult, riot or felony has not taken place". The outcome of this Act was to establish Specials as a permanent feature throughout the war as opposed to being the temporary force of earlier years. In Manchester companies of Specials, each around fifty-strong and commanded by a leader, were assigned to the twenty districts of the city. An inspector of the regular police was in charge of each district. The superintendent of each of the regular police Divisions was in overall command of the Specials on the Division and there was a Special Constables' Administrative Office at the town hall run by Inspector Webster of the City Police.

In addition to foot patrols the Manchester Specials also carried out a number of mounted patrols, the officers acting as traffic police. Where possible a full uniform with peaked cap was provided and for off-duty wear an enamelled lapel badge on civilian clothing was authorised. In addition, many wore a badge inscribed 'On War Duty'. Normally issued to people with reserved occupations, the badge could prevent the presentation of a white feather for cowardice by those misguided members of the public swept away in the patriotic fervour of the early war years.

After the war decorated truncheons were presented to all Specials, bearing the name of the Special Constable and the coat of arms of the city or borough that he served.

In the 1920s, the Specials were largely disbanded although the value of their service was not forgotten and the provisions of the 1914 Act were reinforced by the 1923 Special Constables' Act. This confirmed the permanent nature of the Specials and allowed for the employment of them in naval, military and Air Force yards and stations. It

209. *above*: An instruction from Joseph Nadin dated 14 January 1814 detailing a work rota for Special Constables on No 4 Division in London Road, Manchester.

210a. Special Constabulary uniform worn during the First World War.

also removed some restrictions on the appointment of Specials in Scotland. Also laid down at this time were regulations regarding the reimbursement of out-of-pocket expenses.

However, Specials were enrolled again a few years later during the General Strike of 1926. While civilian volunteers manned buses and the Army provided escorts for food lorries and other supplies, many thousands of Specials were required to help maintain vital services. Many volunteers received no uniform, merely an armband, and after the event decorated truncheons were presented to those who served.

The next great test came during the Second World War when once again the call for volunteers was answered, often by men too old for the Armed services but willing to help out on the home front. Together with a similar group of volunteers, the Police War Reserve who were recruited just for the duration of the war, the Specials 'topped-up' police forces depleted by the enlistment of young officers to the services, and stretched by extra duties such as civil defence, co-ordination of services during air raids and supervision of aliens — friendly or otherwise.

After the war, although the PWR was disbanded, the Specials remained as part of the complement of police forces everywhere and have done so up to the present time.

After joining the Greater Manchester Police, Specials attend a basic recruits course at Sedgley Park in Prestwich. The thorough training includes criminal law, first-aid and traffic regulations. Mock trials and staged accidents help to liven-up training and boost the officer's confidence.

After training they are posted to and organised by Divisions. Specials have tours of duty of about four hours each and deal with similar incidents to the regular police.

Special Constables are not paid but allowances are available and reasonable out-of-pocket expenses are met. A full uniform and equipment are also provided.

210b. *above:* Special Constabulary uniform worn during the First World War. When stocks were not available, Specials improvised a uniform of homburg hats and lapel badges.

211. The No 5 Company of Special Constables in Bolton who served between 1914 and 1917.

212. A testimonial letter from Prime Minister Stanley Baldwin thanking members of the Special Constabulary Reserve for their efforts during the General Strike.

213. *below:* A photograph of Police War Reservist Harry Buxton who acted as the force photographer during the war, taken in the dark-room of Ellison Street police station, Glossop, in 1942.

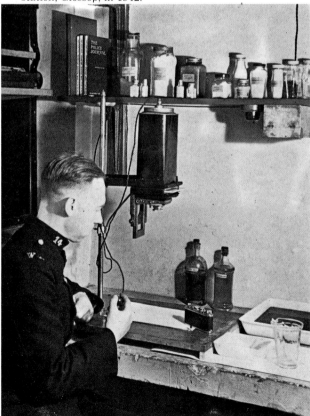

COUNTY BOROUGH OF OLDHAM SPECIAL CONSTABULARY — SENIOR OFFICERS, 1945.

Back Row—Section Commanders A. TRAVIS. H. W. SLACK. R. B. HIRST. W. E. GARTSIDE. H. MELLOR.
Middle Row—Sec. Cdr. E. HILTON. Sec. Cdr. G. C. MEGSON. Dpty. Cmdt. F. DUNKERLEY. Dpty. Cmds. J. S. P. FLEMING. Sec. Cdr. F. MILLS. Sec. Cdrs. V. STOTT and T. SHARPLES.
Front Row—The Commandant. The Chief Constable. Chairman of Watch Committee. Supt. & D. C. C. Dpty. Cmdt. H. B. SHAW. W. F. SCHOFIELD. O.B.E. Alderman A. C. HANSON. J.P. G. MUSGRAVE. G. C. WOOD.

214. *above:* Oldham was typical of many small boroughs whose regular force was greatly expanded by hundreds of volunteers, forming a distinct structure within the police organisation.

215. Recruitment campaigns throughout the years have ensured the maintenance of the Special Constabulary as an integrated part of the police service.

I get great satisfaction out of being a **Special Constable** – and so can you!

JACK HULBERT
COMMANDANT

GREATER MANCHESTER'S POLICEWOMEN

At the end of the nineteenth century, women started to take a much more active role in society than they had done previously.

They began to campaign for the right to vote and began forming societies and organisations such as The National Women's Social and Political Union and the National Union of Women Workers. Some of these women's rights campaigners were later to become early policewomen. The NUWW was one of the many influential pressure groups which pressed Manchester's Watch Committee to employ women police officers. Their requests to the Committee did not have any effect until 1914 when two women were appointed as police assistants. As no city or borough police force was willing to appoint a woman with the full status of a police officer until it had been tried elsewhere, progress was very slow.

During the First World War a number of forces appointed women to act as volunteer patrol officers but they still had no more power than a civilian. In 1919 the Secretary of State thought that the best method of using women was as an aid to the regular police. He felt they would be of greatest help in cases involving women and children.

In Manchester in 1921 nine women were engaged as unofficial police officers to carry out patrol work on the streets. These women also had supervision of women's common lodging houses, and domestic servants registered and occasionally helped obtain evidence in licensing and fortune-telling cases. Policewomen also made enquiries into cases of deserted wives, young single women missing from home and obtained evidence in cases of indecent assault.

Chief Constable Peacock thought that in many respects the work of women police had fallen short of what had been expected. They had not been given the power of arrest but Peacock felt that such a power would add little to their practical ability. The strongest argument used by those who advocated policewomen was that they could deal effectively with prostitution. However, Peacock said that they had shown no success in this area.

Many other Chief Constables had the same feelings about policewomen and so the recruitment of women officers remained a low priority. Despite these set-backs, however, Lancashire County Constabulary appointed two sworn-in women officers in 1921. Oldham Borough appointed one woman, Clara Walkden, in the same year. It was a start.

In 1931 the Home Office set out regulations for policewomen who had been attested (sworn-in). They set down requirements for entrance into the force, the rates of pay and duties they would be expected to perform. The duties were the same as those performed by Manchester's unattested women since 1921. A potential recruit had to be unmarried or a widow, between twenty-two and thirty- five years old and not less than 5ft 4ins in height. A policewoman originally had to resign on marriage, but this was later changed in 1939 when married women were allowed into the force.

The new constable received on appointment fifty shillings per week, rising to a maximum of seventy shillings a week. It was not until 1939 that Manchester finally decided to attest its six women officers and give them full status, the six being finally attested on 18 January 1940. Their uniform consisted of cap, jacket, skirt, white shirt, black tie and black shoes (boots in winter). Due to the good work performed by Manchester's policewomen during World War Two, and because of the changing social conditions and the transference of families to large suburbs, it became apparent that a regular women's police force was essential

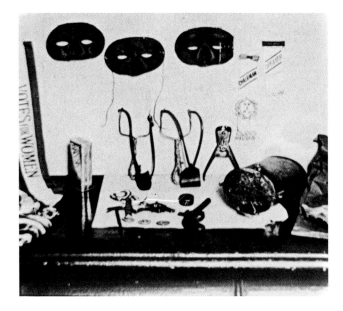

216. *top:* Some of the masks and other paraphernalia recovered during the Suffragette protests.

217. The few women police to venture into an otherwise male-dominated profession were regarded with suspicion by most of the service. It would take many years before they gained acceptance.

to the policing of Manchester.

After the last war Manchester's policewomen numbered twenty-five consisting of one inspector, three sergeants and twenty-one constables. By 1951 the department had increased in size to thirty-four. Despite a higher status, policewomen in the 1950s and 1960s remained a separate

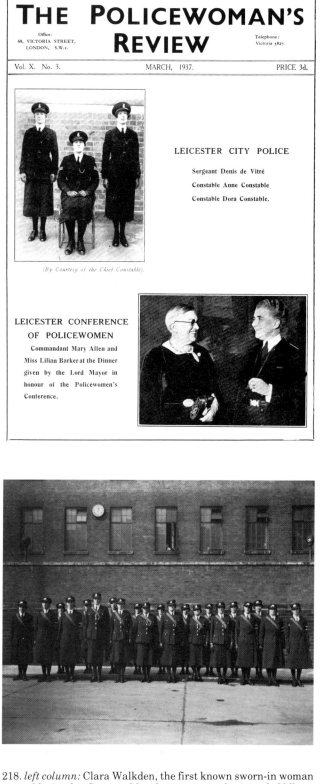

THE **POLICEWOMAN'S** REVIEW

Office:
68, VICTORIA STREET,
LONDON, S.W.1.

Telephone:
Victoria 5827.

Vol. X. No. 3.   MARCH, 1937.   PRICE 3d.

LEICESTER CITY POLICE

Sergeant Denis de Vitré
Constable Anne Constable
Constable Dora Constable.

(By Courtesy of the Chief Constable).

LEICESTER CONFERENCE
OF POLICEWOMEN

Commandant Mary Allen and
Miss Lilian Barker at the Dinner
given by the Lord Mayor in
honour of the Policewomen's
Conference.

Miss Walkden,
POLICEWOMAN.

POLICE OFFICES,
TOWN HALL,
OLDHAM.

TEL. 4041

Form No. 11.
200—28/12/20.

County Borough of Oldham Constabulary.

THIS IS TO CERTIFY THAT

Clara Walkden ~ formerly Police Woman
aged 48 height 5'7½" eyes Brown hair Grey
complexion Fresh a native of Bolton, Lancs.
joined the COUNTY BOROUGH OF OLDHAM CONSTABULARY as a
CONSTABLE on the ~ ninth ~ day of ~ May, 1921 ~
and served till the seventeenth day of ~ June 1943 when she
was pensioned on account of ill-health.
During the above period her conduct was exemplary.

Chief Constable.

Chief Constable's Office,
Oldham. 18th June 1943

Given without erasure.

---

218. *left column:* Clara Walkden, the first known sworn-in woman constable in the Greater Manchester area who joined Oldham Borough in May 1921. She was one of the first officers to have her own visiting card. Note also that even by 1943 the standard leaving certificate was designed only for male officers.

219. *top:* The Policewoman's Review was set up to support and promote the cause of policewomen on a national basis.

220. *above:* Manchester's first six sworn-in policewomen constables, surrounded by members of the Women's Auxiliary Police Corps in January 1940.

department and carried out mainly 'social work' duties. It was not until the 1970s that legislation required women to be treated as equals with men.

Today women are found in all branches of police work and at all levels including that of Chief Officer.

The Women's Auxiliary Police Corps

In November 1939 the Manchester Watch Committee decided to follow Home Office recommendations to appoint a Women's Auxiliary Police Corps (WAPC) to serve alongside the regular women's police force.

Members of the WAPC had to be British subjects, of good character, mentally and physically fit and between the ages of eighteen and fifty-five on enrollment. They were to retire at sixty years of age. The duties of the WAPC were to include the rendering of assistance to the police force in matters such as driving, maintaining and repairing motor vehicles, clerical work including typing and shorthand, plus telephone, wireless and canteen work.

Service in wartime was generally part-time and unpaid but a few were chosen to be full-time paid auxiliaries at the rate of forty shillings per week. The women were not classed as Special Constables but were seen instead as part of the civil defence service.

The approval to authorise the strength of the WAPC lay with the Secretary of State, and he gave Manchester permission to employ between fifteen and twenty full-time auxiliaries. On 15 February 1940 the WAPC, which numbered fifteen, was sworn-in and five more joined at a later date.

The uniform of the WAPC was a blue gabardine waterproof coat with belt, a blue peaked cap, gauntlet gloves, a blue cotton overall for indoor wear, an armlet or breast badge with WAPC on it and a monogram. The armlet was to be of blue cloth, 3ins wide with two strips of white cloth half an inch wide sewn along the top and bottom edges,

221. *above:* School crossing patrol, office work and cases involving women and children formed the staple duties of policewomen in the 1950s and 1960s.

222. *top right:* A well-earned break for PW Jackie Franklin-Grey (centre) and colleagues.

223. *middle right:* Salford City police officer with a member of the Women's Auxiliary Police Corps (WAPC) circa 1940.

224. Margaret Gornall, GMP's only woman Chief Superintendent, who presently commands the Police Personnel Department.

with the monogram WAPC enclosed in an oval measuring 2.5ins x 1.5ins.

The Manchester Chief Constable in 1939, John Maxwell, was interviewed by the *Manchester Guardian* on 17 November that year regarding the WAPC. Mr Maxwell pointed out that, since the outbreak of the Second World War, a problem had arisen connected with the establishment of military training centres which had been set up in various parts of the city. Mr Maxwell thought that it was only natural that such centres had attracted the presence of undesirables and that it was essentially a job for women to deal with crimes involving women or causes of public annoyance involving prostitutes. He thought that the suggestion of the Government to form the WAPC was a suitable expedient to meet the difficulties caused by the camps, as both the cause and the effect would disappear when the war was over.

In 1946 it was decided to disband the WAPC as their purpose in patrolling the camps was over. However, they had performed their duties so well that the new Chief Constable of Manchester, Joseph Bell, told the Watch Committee that, for the purposes of policing Manchester properly, fifteen members of the WAPC should be transferred to the regular police force and that the Secretary of State should be asked to approve the transfer. This was duly done and the length of service of the remaining WAPC members was extended along with the Police War Reserve until they were finally disbanded in September 1948.

POLICING DURING THE WARS

The First World War

The outbreak of the war was greeted with enthusiasm by many sections of the community, who saw it as an opportunity to serve their country in what was anticipated to be a short and heroic conflict. The police were to feel the impact of the momentous events almost immediately as the ex-soldiers amongst them were recalled to their regiments. Even though there would be no conscription until 1916, many police officers volunteered for service, further depleting the ranks. In response to this, Special Constables were enrolled in great numbers.

The careful supervision of foreigners was a task entrusted to the police and initially this was simply a matter of escorting out enemy aliens when war was declared and ensuring that friendly aliens carried their internal passport. However, in Manchester events took a more violent turn.

After the sinking of the liner *Lusitania* by a German U-boat, anti-German rioting broke out in the city, and a mob turned its fury on any shop with a German-sounding proprietor. As is often the case, the victims were mainly naturalised Germans or second generation immigrants. Windows were broken and a pork butcher's shop ransacked.

Later in the war the police had a foretaste of the air raids to come in the Second World War. Although the zeppelin airships carried only a small load of bombs and the raids were meant more to inspire terror than cause economic disruption, the raids in London caused widespread fear and panic as, for the first time, civilians were brought into the front line.

In 1916 Bolton was raided by zeppelins. Thirteen people were killed as bombs fell in the Kirk Street, Deane Road and Parrott Street areas of the town. Although a great tragedy, the damage sustained in the raid would appear light when compared with the "blitz" of the 1939-45 war.

225. Manchester Police serving in the Grenadier Guards, taken in May 1915.

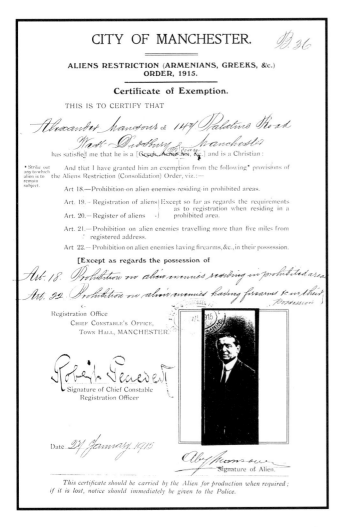

The Justice of the Peace having in a loud voice commanded, or caused to be commanded silence to be, while Proclamation is making, shall openly and with loud voice make, or cause to be made Proclamation in these words or like in effect :

"OUR SOVEREIGN LORD THE KING,

"chargeth and commandeth all Persons,
"being assembled, immediately to disperse
"themselves, and peaceably to depart to
"their habitations, or to their lawful
"business, upon the pains contained in the
" Act made in the first Year of King George for
" preventing tumults and riotous assemblies."

"GOD SAVE THE KING."

The Second World War

The greatest test the police of Britain had to face was that of aerial bombardment.

The first bombs to fall in the Greater Manchester area were dropped from an off-course single aircraft on 29 July 1940. A small deliberate raid followed on 8 August that year with both high-explosive and incendiary bombs being dropped. This small raid was long to be remembered, however, as the Salford Police suffered its first casualty. A policeman on duty outside the Civil Defence Report and Control Centre was injured by a falling bundle of propaganda leaflets entitled *Hitler's Last Appeal To Reason*. The officer's comments are not recorded!

Whilst the impression of those early war years was that of improvisation and 'muddling through', in one area at least, several years' preparation was finally coming to the test. The Air Raid Precautions' Act of 1937 allowed the building of a framework of civil defence workers. The police service was also prepared and in the years leading up to the war, Chief Constables were well-briefed on the likely effects of a bombing campaign.

Even today it cannot be fully appreciated what horrors they felt awaited them. Due to the weight given to the unfortunate catch phrase of the 1930s, "the bomber will always get through", the authorities steeled themselves for wholesale destruction by wave after wave of heavy bombers. Thousands of civilian casualties were expected on the first day. Grim preparations were made — it is believed that tens of thousands of wax paper folded coffins were secretly prepared, and plans were laid for the dumping of the dead in the North Sea. As well as ordinary bombs, there was strong evidence that poison gas would also be used, causing many more to die.

Expecting the worst, the civil defence teams were 'broken in' by small raids through the summer and autumn of 1940. The heaviest raid came in December that year during the nights of 22nd and 23rd December. It was not immediately clear whether the bombers were heading for Manchester or Liverpool, the latter having been raided on the 20th and 21st of that month. The raiders massed over Manchester and during the two nights over 288 high-explosive bombs and countless numbers of incendiaries fell, killing over 360 people and injuring 1,180. Around 200 businesses, 165 warehouses, 150 offices and 5 banks were destroyed. Over 30,000 houses in the Manchester area were damaged, with thousands made homeless.

Many firemen and police worked through the forty-eight hours and it was not until Christmas Day that the regional controllers could report that the area was under control. At one point nearly all of Piccadilly was ablaze and several buildings were demolished to create firebreaks.

The local police, who were out during raids fire-watching, protecting damaged buildings from looting and ensuring communications were maintained, were reinforced under a pre-arranged scheme. Alongside regular officers, including many whose retirement had been suspended for the duration of the war, were thousands of Special Constables and Police War Reserve officers and Womens' Auxiliary Police Corps

226. *top:* A Certificate of Exemption for Alexander Mansour, of Syrian nationality.

227.*middle:* 'Reading the Riot Act' — an actual copy of the Proclamation read to the crowd by a JP or representative.

228. *left:* The Great War was the first time the civilian population directly experienced the shock of war on their own doorsteps — as seen here in Parrott Street, Bolton.

members made up of civilians drafted-in as volunteers. Although still civilian they supplemented tasks carried out by the regular police and patrolled the newly-formed Army training camps where the large numbers of conscripted men were gathered. The camps had attracted the less than desirable elements of society offering black-market goods, drink and prostitution. The creation of the WAPC also spurred on the move to appoint additional sworn-in policewomen constables. Many other boroughs followed suit and, although intended only as a wartime measure, they were retained after the war with some members going on to serve in the regular police.

The Stretford area was to be on the receiving end of many bombing raids during the war, including one which devastated the East Union Street police station. A total of eleven officers, including members of the Special Constabulary, were killed during the attacks on 23-26 December 1941 and 11-12 March 1941, one of them being killed near to Stretford Library in King Street. The target was the docks and industrial area around Trafford Park and at one stage communications with the area were only maintained through the use of a police radio car. In a further raid in June 1941 the old Victorian Assize Courts at Strangeways were gutted. Also hit that time was the Manchester City Police headquarters at Southmill Street. Although two members of the civil defence messenger service were killed, women on duty in the control centre continued their duties with great calmness and courage.

Manchester itself was to suffer further raids until August 1942, when a lull occurred. During that time sixty-four men and women in the police, fire and civil defence services had been killed and about 250 injured.

The final chapter in Greater Manchester's wartime experiences came just before dawn on 24 December 1944, four years after the great Manchester blitz. Fifty German aircraft took off from coastal airfields. Each carried a V1 pilotless guided missile and off Skegness they released their bombs. That morning thirty of the bombs crossed the coast. Each was fitted with a primitive guidance system and a device which cut out the jet engine after a calculated travel time. Eleven fell within fifteen miles of their target — Manchester. A further six fell within ten miles in the outer suburbs. One landed in the city limits. Another landed in the Chapel Street area of Tottington, near Bury, which killed seven people and injured fourteen more.

Surprisingly, at this final stage of the war, some of these VI's ejected propaganda leaflets as they fell, the leaflet carrying a purported facsimile of a letter from an allied POW in Germany.

Among many extra tasks placed on the shoulders of the police during the last war was supervision of the National Registration Scheme. Identity cards were carried by all the

229. *below:* School gas mask drill became part of the normal life for Manchester children, as depicted here in 1938. Older children who joined the Civil Defence Services took part in full-scale gas alerts.

230. *opposite page:* Those people not immediately eligible for conscription were encouraged to join a number of organisations which were enlarged or specially set up to meet the emergency.

YOU CAN'T BE CERTAIN
—YOU CAN BE READY

JOIN YOUR LOCAL
SPECIAL CONSTABULARY

ASK AT ANY POLICE STATION

ISSUED BY H.M. GOVERNMENT

A7441 Wt. 23593 38,500 9/51 Gp. 961 Fosh & Cross Ltd., London.

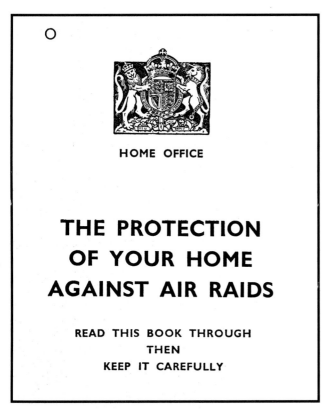

HOME OFFICE

THE PROTECTION OF YOUR HOME AGAINST AIR RAIDS

READ THIS BOOK THROUGH

THEN

KEEP IT CAREFULLY

231. *above:* One of many Home Office booklets aimed at informing the general public about the risks of air raids. This one advised on choosing a suitable 'refuge room', protection from gas attacks and other emergency measures.

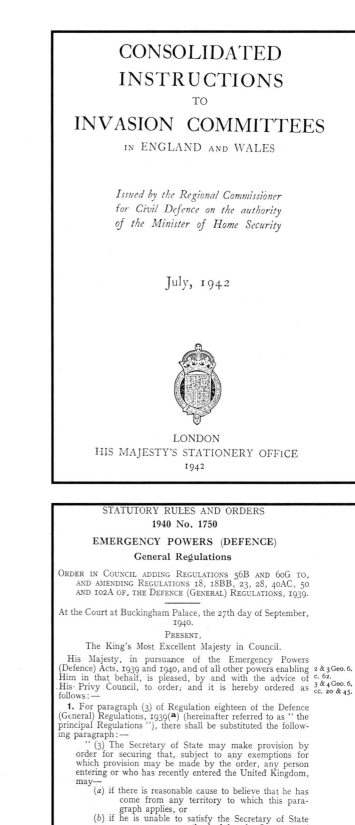

CONSOLIDATED INSTRUCTIONS
TO
INVASION COMMITTEES
IN ENGLAND AND WALES

Issued by the Regional Commissioner for Civil Defence on the authority of the Minister of Home Security

July, 1942

LONDON
HIS MAJESTY'S STATIONERY OFFICE
1942

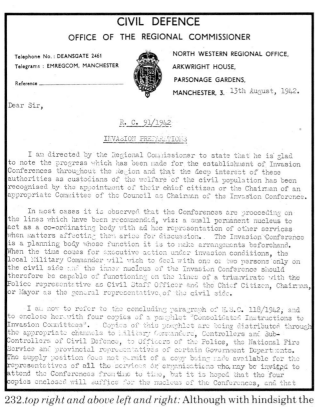

CIVIL DEFENCE

OFFICE OF THE REGIONAL COMMISSIONER

Telephone No.: DEANSGATE 2461
Telegrams: EMREGCOM, MANCHESTER

NORTH WESTERN REGIONAL OFFICE,
ARKWRIGHT HOUSE,
PARSONAGE GARDENS,
MANCHESTER, 3. 13th August, 1942.

Reference _____

Dear Sir,

R. C. 91/1942

INVASION PREPARATIONS

I am directed by the Regional Commissioner to state that he is glad to note the progress which has been made for the establishment of Invasion Conferences throughout the Region and that the deep interest of these authorities as custodians of the welfare of the civil population has been recognised by the appointment of their chief citizen or the Chairman of an appropriate Committee of the Council as Chairman of the Invasion Conference.

In most cases it is observed that the Conferences are proceeding on the lines which have been recommended, viz: a small permanent nucleus to act as a co-ordinating body with ad hoc representation of other services when matters affecting them arise for discussion. The Invasion Conference is a planning body whose function it is to make arrangements beforehand. When the time comes for executive action under invasion conditions, the local Military Commander will wish to deal with one or two persons only on the civil side and the inner nucleus of the Invasion Conference should therefore be capable of functioning on the lines of a triumvirate with the Police representative as Civil Staff Officer and the Chief Citizen, Chairman, or Mayor as the general representative of the civil side.

I am now to refer to the concluding paragraph of H.S.C. 118/1942, and to enclose herewith four copies of a pamphlet "Consolidated Instructions to Invasion Committees". Copies of this pamphlet are being distributed through the appropriate channels to Military Commanders, Controllers and Sub-Controllers of Civil Defence, to Officers of the Police, the National Fire Service and provincial representatives of certain Government Departments. The supply position does not permit of a copy being made available for the representatives of all the services or organisations who may be invited to attend the Conferences from time to time, but it is hoped that the four copies enclosed will suffice for the nucleus of the Conferences, and that

232.*top right and above left and right:* Although with hindsight the threat of invasion diminished after 1941, preparations continued to be made.

STATUTORY RULES AND ORDERS
1940 No. 1750

EMERGENCY POWERS (DEFENCE)
General Regulations

ORDER IN COUNCIL ADDING REGULATIONS 56B AND 60G TO, AND AMENDING REGULATIONS 18, 18BB, 23, 28, 40AC, 50 AND 102A OF, THE DEFENCE (GENERAL) REGULATIONS, 1939.

At the Court at Buckingham Palace, the 27th day of September, 1940.

PRESENT,

The King's Most Excellent Majesty in Council.

His Majesty, in pursuance of the Emergency Powers (Defence) Acts, 1939 and 1940, and of all other powers enabling Him in that behalf, is pleased, by and with the advice of His Privy Council, to order; and it is hereby ordered as follows:— [2 & 3 Geo. 6. c. 62. 3 & 4 Geo. 6. cc. 20 & 45.]

1. For paragraph (3) of Regulation eighteen of the Defence (General) Regulations, 1939(a) (hereinafter referred to as " the principal Regulations "), there shall be substituted the following paragraph:—

"(3) The Secretary of State may make provision by order for securing that, subject to any exemptions for which provision may be made by the order, any person entering or who has recently entered the United Kingdom, may—

(a) if there is reasonable cause to believe that he has come from any territory to which this paragraph applies, or

(b) if he is unable to satisfy the Secretary of State or any person authorised by the Secretary of State in that behalf as to his identity or as to the purpose for which he is entering or has entered the United Kingdom,

be detained pending inquiries, or be required, pending inquiries, to notify his movements in such manner and at such times and to such authority or person as may be specified in the order."

233. These pictures show scenes of devastation which largely affected the inner suburbs of Manchester and Salford. Note the police pillar withstood Hitler's onslaught!

234. The dull red glow from Piccadilly could be seen from miles around.

population and were issued at birth. The ones carried by police officers and other officials bore a photograph. A police officer in uniform could demand to see the card of anyone that was stopped. Failure to produce a card meant the issue of a form which instructed the individual to report to a given police station within two days or face a severe penalty. It is clear, however, that the ordinary card, without photograph, could be the subject of abuse and indeed, following the murder of a prostitute named Olive Balchin in Manchester in 1946, she was found to be carrying two cards with different names.

While more the preserve of M15 or the Special Branch, ordinary police were nevertheless involved in the supervision of aliens in the country and the detection of spies. Routine police enquiries paid off in one case in Manchester involving an official of the Air Ministry and a German girl. All aliens accepted into Britain as refugees had, by law, to notify the police of any change in their address. A German girl living in Macclesfield had moved to Didsbury and was living with an Air Ministry official named William Downing. She had not informed the police of her move. When the Manchester Police finally found her in Didsbury and made a search of the house, it was discovered that Downing had photographed a badge worn by aircraft inspectors, an Air Ministry pass and a permit to enter prohibited areas. Downing was found guilty of assisting the enemy and was sent to prison for six years. The girl was interned for the rest of the war.

Rationing and the shortage of goods led many to theft and offering goods on the black-market. At one point a Manchester detective, Daniel Timpany, declared that the theft and re-sale of black-market petrol was becoming a

racket. There was also a trade in stolen clothing coupons. While many people sold their coupons to others for cash, a thirty-one-year old woman in Manchester was sent to prison for dealing in stolen coupons and for organising burglaries by two twelve-year old boys. On a more serious note there were cases of children vandalising and looting bombed houses. In Manchester a man was goaled for receiving stolen goods from a ten year old boy.

Tragically, the easier access to firearms and munitions for the criminally-minded led to several deaths in the Greater Manchester area. Four boys from Burnage in Manchester were killed when they tampered with unexploded shells they had found while on a cycling trip in Staffordshire and had then brought home for closer examination. A soldier intervening in a fight between two men outside the Unicorn Inn in Hulme, Manchester, loaded his rifle, which then went off accidentally. The single bullet that was fired passed through two women, killing them instantly and went on to wound two other people.

The region was, however, stunned by the deaths of Detective Sergeant Dale and Detective Inspector Stables of the Rochdale Borough Police who were blown up on 20 March 1941 while they investigated a house in the town. A teenager had stolen firearms and ammunition from a local arms dump and concealed them in a box in the cellar of his home. The box was booby-trapped and, while executing a search warrant, the two detectives opened the box setting off explosives. Two other detectives were injured and the boy's father lost an eye.

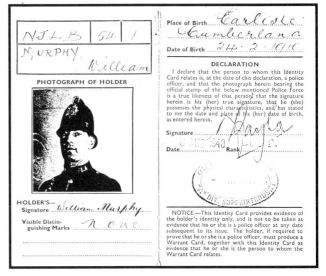

235. *top:* Members of the Ashton-under-Lyne Police Auxiliary Messenger Service.

236. *left:* An enrolment notice for the Police War Reserve.

237. *above:* A wartime police identity card.

The following is the list of prohibited items given in the CONTROL OF PHOTOGRAPHY ORDER (No. 1) 1939 dated Sept. 10th 1939

Fortifications, battery, searchlight, listening post or other work of defence
Aerodrome or seaplane station.
Assembly of forces.
Barracks or encampment.
Arsenal, factory, magazine or store for munitions of war, arms, equipment, or supplies for the forces
Wireless, telegraph, telephone, signal or cable station.
Dock, caisson, dockyard, harbour, shipbuilding works or loading pier.
Vessel of war or any vessel or vehicle engaged in the transport of supplies or personnel.
Aircraft or the wreckage of any aircraft.
Building, structure, vessel or other object damaged by enemy action or as a result of steps taken to repel enemy action.
Hospital or station at which casualties whether civil or otherwise, are treated.
Any ambulance or convoy of injured persons or any injured.
Electricity, gas or water works, or any gasometer or reservoir, or any oil store.
Assembly of persons for transport or evacuation or any temporary camp or other accommodation or transport vehicles used for evacuation.
Riotous or disorderly assembly, or premises or other objects damaged in the course of such an assembly.
Any roads or railways exclusively connected with works of defence.

Printed by John Swain & Son Ltd London

PHOTOGRAPHY AS USUAL

Extract from War Office Announcement re photography

Dated 7th February 1940

" Generally there is no ban upon the carriage of cameras in public places by persons other than enemy aliens, who would require a permit for this purpose. It is not forbidden to photograph views or objects except those expressly prohibited items contained in the Orders "

Please carry this card with you to show should you be questioned when using your camera.

8th June, 1946

TO-DAY, AS WE CELEBRATE VICTORY, I send this personal message to you and all other boys and girls at school. For you have shared in the hardships and dangers of a total war and you have shared no less in the triumph of the Allied Nations.

I know you will always feel proud to belong to a country which was capable of such supreme effort; proud, too, of parents and elder brothers and sisters who by their courage, endurance and enterprise brought victory. May these qualities be yours as you grow up and join in the common effort to establish among the nations of the world unity and peace.

George R.I.

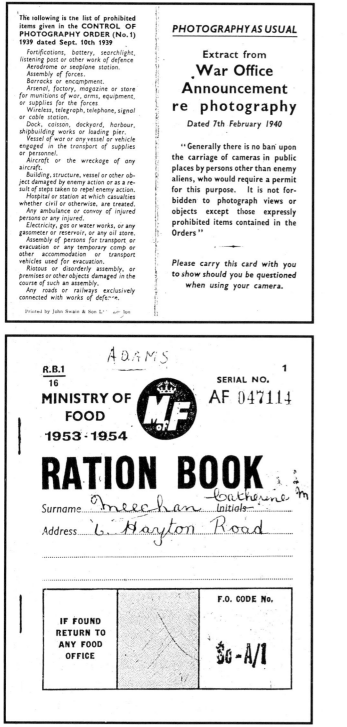

R.B.1 / 16
1
MINISTRY OF FOOD
1953·1954

SERIAL NO.
AF 047114

ADAMS

RATION BOOK

Surname ...Meechan... Initials ...Catherine M...
Address ...6 Hayton Road...

IF FOUND RETURN TO ANY FOOD OFFICE		F.O. CODE No. 36-A/1

238. *top left:* The 'Photography as Usual' card advised photographers on what they could and could not photograph during the war.

239. *above and right*: Rationing items such as food, clothing and petrol continued into the 1950s from which time these examples date.

240. *top right:* King George VI sending heartfelt thanks to the children of Britain.

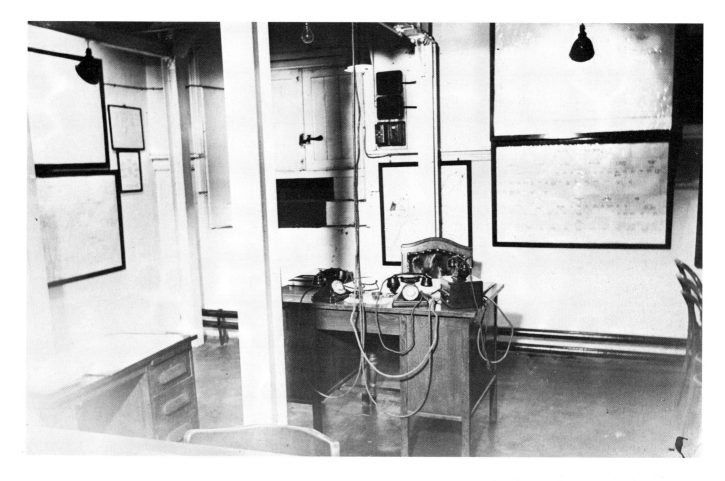

241a-b. The ARP Control Centre (above) from which information about imminent raids would be relayed to the public from air raid sirens placed on police and public buildings.

Spreading the Word

Work, Rest and Play

Fresh air, exercise and an active social life have always been a very important way of relaxing from the stresses and strains of every-day working life. Nowhere is this more true than in the police service and the forces which now make up Greater Manchester Police have a long tradition of encouraging rest and play.

A police officer on duty never knows what each day will bring or what he will be called upon to do. Taking an active part in various forms of sport and leisure helps him to deal with whatever comes his way — whether rescuing a drowning child, chasing a criminal or defending himself during an attack.

Find a comfortable chair, put your feet up and relax whilst you look at how police officers from yesteryear enjoyed some of their pastimes . . .

Amateur Swimming Association

PRESENTED TO

Oldham Police S.C.

FOR

winning the
Club Team Swimming Championship of England,
1929.

Reginald A. Colwell   President.

_____   Hon. Treasurer.

_____   Hon. Secretary.

1268

S.F.D.

GMP's 'Tardis'

The police museum occupies the old Newton Street police station which was completed in October 1879. The station was designed by a Mr Lynde and built by a Mr Foggatt. It was operational for 99 years and served as a section station for part of the Manchester City Police 'A' Division which covered the city centre.

For many years it was one of the busiest stations in Manchester. The original entrance was on Friday, later Faraday, Street and therefore the station was sometimes known by that name.

Shortly after the station closed the task of creating a force museum was begun by personnel from the Greater Manchester Police.

Where To Find Us

Visiting Times

All visits to the Greater Manchester Police Museum are by appointment only.

For details telephone: 061-855 3290

or write to:

The Curator
Greater Manchester Police Museum
Newton Street
Manchester
M1 1ES

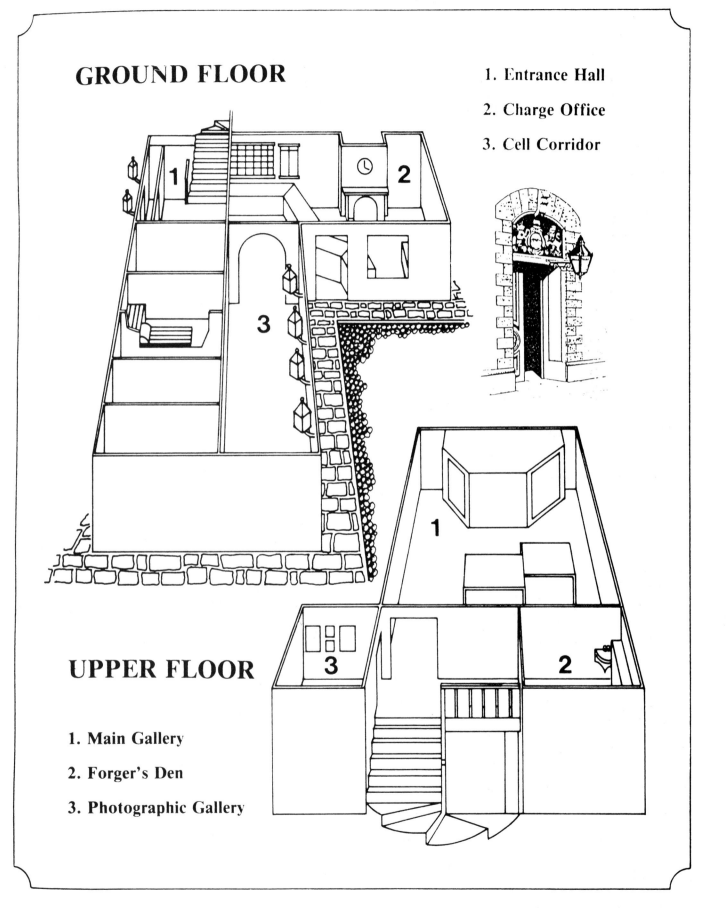

GROUND FLOOR

1. Entrance Hall
2. Charge Office
3. Cell Corridor

UPPER FLOOR

1. Main Gallery
2. Forger's Den
3. Photographic Gallery

Acknowledgements

Book produced by Duncan Broady, Museum Curator, and Carol Sawkill, Public Relations Officer, Greater Manchester Police.

GMP would like to acknowledge their appreciation to the undermentioned who allowed them to use some of the photographs contained herein:

Greater Manchester Police

Publicity Photographic Unit
General Photographic Unit
Sgt P Garnett
Mr B Smith
Rochdale Police Museum
Oldham Police Museum

Libraries

Bury Libraries and Arts Departments
Manchester Public Libraries: Local History Section
Oldham Metropolitan Borough Council:
Local Studies Department.
Rochdale Metropolitan Borough Council
Salford Local History Library
Stockport Local Studies Library
Tameside Local Studies Library

Newspapers

Ashton Reporter Group
Bolton Evening News

Manchester Evening News
Oldham Evening Chronicle
Stockport Express Advertiser and Times

Miscellaneous

Mr T Brown
Central Office of Information
Mr W Challoner
Norman Edwards Associates (Manchester) Ltd
Mr R J Goslin
Home Office
Longdendale Amenity Society
National Portrait Gallery
Mr E H Oakes
Police Review Publishing Company
Sky Views and General Ltd
Miss D Wildgoose

NARPO Members

Mrs H Egerton
Mr C H Hardisty
Mr W Johnstone
Mr B Stephens
Mrs A Stephenson

259. Proclamation of King Edward VIII in 1933 — strike up the band!

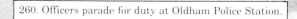

261. Kim assisting handlers PC Ogden and PC Goodfellow of Rochdale in 1953.